Notes & Apologies:

✶ Subscriptions to *The Believer* include four issues, one of which
themed and may come with a bonus item, such as a giant poster or art object.
View our subscription deals online at *thebeliever.net/subscribe*.

✶ The incidental illustrations in this issue, of two-toned lapidary flora, are by
Matthew Houston.

✶ Tetiana Yanukova, whose illustrations accompany Dave Eggers's "Sketches
from Ukraine" (page 74), is an award-winning artist based in Kyiv. When
Dave was in Ukraine, they met up at a café in downtown Kyiv. Before the war,
she said, she received commissions from a wide variety of commercial clients
from around the world, but today her work has largely dried up. "There
were several times," she told him, "when potential clients asked me where
I'm based, and when I told them Ukraine, they ghosted me." One of her
remaining clients, from Japan, added a clause indicating where compensation
should be sent if she were to be killed in the war. Rest assured, Tetiana is fine,
and is very happy to be contacted about commissions. For those interested in
seeing more of her work, her handle on Instagram is @anni_tett.

✶ Alexander Chee microinterviews Wo Chan on pages 8, 28, 61, 100, 103, and
112. Chan is a poet and drag artist who performs as The Illustrious Pearl.
Their debut book of poetry, *Togetherness*, is available from Nightboat Books.

✶ Our friend Paul La Farge passed away on January 18, 2023. He was the author
of four dazzling novels, most recently *The Night Ocean* (2017), and *The Facts
of Winter*, a series of fictional dreams (published by McSweeney's). He was
also a brilliant essayist, and wrote frequently for us over the years. Paul was,
in fact, one of the first writers we asked to contribute to *The Believer*, and his
piece in our debut issue (March 2003), "The Little Nicholson Baker inside
My Head," helped establish the tone for the magazine's literary essays: erudite,
curious, entertaining. His next essay, "Destroy All Monsters" (September
2006), was an epic—a long and playfully bifurcated piece that served as both
a fascinating history of Dungeons & Dragons and a tender, hilarious account
of traveling to Wisconsin with a friend to play a session of the game with
Gary Gygax, its legendary cocreator. His most recent *Believer* article, from
2013, was a typically elegant and wide-ranging essay that drew connections
between Baron Haussmann's remaking of Paris in the nineteenth century,
the uncanny stillness generated by noise-canceling headphones, and an
unfinished Kafka story, to give the reader a "mole's eye view" of the novel.
Each piece he wrote—from ten, from twenty years ago—gives the same
pleasure now as it did upon publication; and releases a new sorrow.

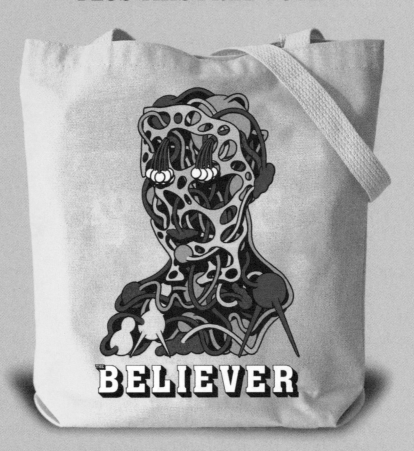

DEAR THE BELIEVER

849 VALENCIA STREET, SAN FRANCISCO, CA 94110

letters@thebeliever.net

Dear Believer,

I'm writing, mostly, to let you all know what I've been up to while you've been restarting this magazine. Writing because inside the prisons I visit, I've witnessed all the places the stories we write and edit don't go. Writing because I met a woman just the other day who said to me, "I've been locked up for thirty-six years," longer than the life of two of the folks on my team. I'm writing, too, because I didn't weep, but this one woman did in front of me, as she stared at the cherry bookshelves and hundreds of books placed on them that created a library where there had once been just a collection of cells. Alas, there is always more to say than there are words. But let me tell you about my past few days, if you'll indulge my overreach.

Freedom Reads opens libraries in prisons. We bring bookshelves made of maple or cherry or oak into prison housing units, each set with five hundred books. The libraries are forty-four inches high and curved and the books are accessible from both sides. I designed them with the architects at MASS Design, and without a doubt, from the curving shape to the finger joints to the wood, they are the most beautiful objects in any prison in America.

The other day, we opened twenty-one libraries in California prisons, which is to say we brought beauty and more than ten thousand books to what many told us had felt like a barren landscape of ripped pages and dated novels before we arrived. So many times I looked in the eyes of the men and women there and thought: My g-d, you are too beautiful to be here. And I felt bad, a bit, because I'd then notice the injured, the disabled, the troubled, and realize that they, too, were far too lovely for what prisons make us endure. As an aside, I should say that there were these holding cells. Portable. Fit for one person. Like a cage for a rat. And each time I walked past them, I shivered. But I did not weep, because, well, there are things that you no longer weep for.

We'd started this whole business days earlier, loading an 18-wheeler with more than 110 bookshelves and benches at 2666 State Street. We call our spot Bolaño's House, for obvious reasons. After loading the truck, Tyler and Claire flew to Fresno early to meet the libraries as they arrived. James Washington, Chris Spruill, and Doug Harmon came in from Louisiana to help with the final preparation of the bookshelves before we loaded them onto a Penske truck and headed to the prisons. James was outside of Louisiana for the first time. With Doug, he drove out to see the Sequoias and the wreckage that flooding had done to the landscape.

Valley State Prison is sprawling. Four yards, each with four housing units. Tyler drove the Penske from unit to unit and we all unloaded the shelves together: prisoners, us, staff. As we walked around, folks would stop us and say: "Y'all brought those libraries? Beautiful, beautiful." They'd say: "And the books, I hear they're good too." Every stop was like an English class discussion. "I've been wanting to read *Hamlet*. What's it about?" "It's a tragedy. What do you think?" Someone, seemingly everyone, kept talking about *The Count of Monte Cristo*. Kept grabbing books they'd read and remembered.

And they'd done so much time. Twenty years and thirty years and thirty-six years. One woman, who was being released soon, after eighteen years, asked if she could donate books. I explained that we used only new books and she was like, "I'll give you new books." Then I said, "Why don't you come back with us and open more libraries?" She was incredulous. Explained how she'd done eighteen years, that they wouldn't let her back in. I told her James's story, how he did twenty-five years in Angola and three months after his release was back inside with us and the libraries he'd built. She turned to her friend and smiled.

Last night I did my solo show for more than one hundred guys at VSP. We talked about what it means to go inside a lot. After the show, I answered questions for an hour, signed books, heard more stories. And of course this isn't the half of it. But it's all a reminder of why reading and writing are absolutely singular.

And now I'm on a flight home.
Take care,
Reginald Dwayne Betts
Founder and Director, Freedom Reads
New Haven, CT

> THINK ABOUT KAFKA—HE ALMOST NEVER FINISHED ANYTHING.
>
> *p. 62*

> SHOULD I FORCE MY DOG TO WALK IN THE RAIN?
>
> *p. 20*

Portrait illustrations by Kristian Hammerstad; cockroach illustrations by Kyle Hilton

ART-MAKING
AND THE
MARKET ARE
AT ODDS. *p. 102*

IN 1969, MY GRAND-
MOTHER TRIED TO
DECAPITATE HER GOOD
FRIEND ELLA WINTER. *p. 36*

Photo by Rebecca Rukeyser; rock illustration by Madison Ketcham; plant illustrations by Andrea Settimo

RESURRECTOR

A ROTATING GUEST COLUMN IN WHICH WRITERS REEXAMINE CRITICALLY
UNACCLAIMED WORKS OF ART. IN THIS ISSUE: *ISHTAR* (1987)

by Brandon Hobson

The 1987 film *Ishtar* opens with two middle-aged men sitting at a piano. Lyle Rogers (Warren Beatty) and Chuck Clarke (Dustin Hoffman) are trying to write a song called "Dangerous Business," which Clarke later tells Rogers is as good as anything Simon and Garfunkel wrote. In that opening scene, the two flub along as they try to compose the song's lyrics: "Telling the truth is a bad idea. / Telling the truth is a scary predicament. / Telling the truth is a bitter herb. / When you get out of that tunnel… it's a bitter herb."

"Forget *herb*," Hoffman says in frustration. "I've never heard of a hit with the word *herb* in it."

I first saw the film on a homemade VHS tape with poor tracking. My brother had recorded the movie from Cinemax or somewhere, and by the time I got to college it had become regular viewing on nights when someone had booze or pot. Despite our age difference, I identified with Beatty's and Hoffman's characters in their struggle to write—one of the reasons the film's opening is so humorous. By college I had begun writing stories, and like those two men, I naively thought something I had written was good when it was, in fact, terrible. But my appreciation for *Ishtar* grew with numerous viewings.

More than the adventure comedy it's labeled as, *Ishtar* is actually a genre-exploder, full of ingenious one-liners; a propulsive, smart narrative/plot; and a subliminal de lunatico inquirendo that renders a swift kick to the psychic penetralia. Written by Elaine May, whose work also includes *The Birdcage* and *Tootsie*, this film delivers in large doses. The attempts Beatty's and Hoffman's characters make to survive life-threatening situations are perfunctory and funny and garner empathy from the audience; love interests, trust, friendship, and survival remain constant and compelling themes throughout.

The headline in good old Gene Siskel's May 14, 1987, review in *The Chicago Tribune* reads: NOTHING WORKS IN BORING "ISHTAR," and Siskel even doubles down with the inexorable claim that the film "*fails at every level*" (italics mine), an assessment that I, of course, wholeheartedly disagree with. Most if not all the reviews were poor. They failed to see and appreciate the humor and pacing of the film. What critics like Siskel saw as pacing problems are in fact part of the film's "ineluctable modality of the visible," as James Joyce would say. They are less gratuitous and more steeped in following the path toward redemption: two men—single, lonely, damaged, broke, pathetically pusillanimous, desperate to write and sell poorly written songs—flee to the fictional country of Ishtar, near Morocco, to perform a gig, but instead become involved, unwillingly and by accident, with the CIA in an attempt to overthrow the monarch of Ishtar.

Film nerds of the world, unite! The exformative associations the movie creates are what are most appealing to those of us who attempt to create things like art. Largely through unsubtle humor and empathy, the movie reveals the truths we fail to recognize in ourselves until much later—like trying to write songs or stories or poems or whatever; none are as great as we seem to believe they are in the moment. True greatness moves through a sort of coeval time, persists, survives, and thrives many years later. I recently rewatched the movie and found it as funny, smart, and enjoyable as I did so many years ago, even minus the weed. ✯

Illustration by Andrea Settimo

STUFF I'VE BEEN READING

A QUARTERLY COLUMN, STEADY AS EVER

by Nick Hornby

BOOKS READ:

✶ *The Critic's Daughter*—
Priscilla Gilman
✶ *Monsters: A Fan's
Dilemma*—Claire Dederer
✶ *Busy Being Free: A Lifelong Romantic
Is Seduced by Solitude*—Emma Forrest
✶ *Tomorrow, and Tomorrow, and
Tomorrow*—Gabrielle Zevin
✶ *Lucy by the Sea*—Elizabeth Strout

BOOKS BOUGHT:

✶ *Dilla Time: The Life and Afterlife of
J Dilla, the Hip-Hop Producer Who
Reinvented Rhythm*—Dan Charnas
✶ *An Autobiography: And Other
Writings*—Anthony Trollope
✶ *The Philosophy of Modern
Song*—Bob Dylan
✶ *The Rabbit Hutch*—Tess Gunty
✶ *National Treasures: Saving the
Nation's Art in World War II*—
Caroline Shenton

I s a man ever going to write a good book again? Or rather: Is a man ever going to write a book that I actually want to read? Or are we finished as a gender? We had our time: Dickens, Kurt Vonnegut, Zane Grey, a bunch of others whose names I cannot remember… Oh, I'm just sucking up to you. I'm guessing that you're either a woman, or a man who is fed up with men, and I can't blame you. We've had a bad twenty-first century. And in any case, I have read a very good book by a man recently, but I've left him out because I couldn't have started this column the way I did if I'd included him. *The Believer* is now a quarterly, so I can be, *have* to be, selective in the books I choose to write about here; I can, if I want, turn myself into any kind of

reader I want to be. Next issue, this column might be full of novels written by people who have donated a kidney, and, once again, I will appear both superior and empathetic.

But it is true that I am more drawn to books by women at the stage of life I'm currently traveling through with alarming speed, before arriving somewhere I probably won't want to be. Why is that? It's not like these books have anything else in common: there's a brilliant work of criticism, beautiful memoirs that do not resemble each other in tone or in subject matter, and two novels that could not be more unalike if they had come to us from Mars and Venus. (Younger readers: this is a reference to a popular book from the late twentieth century that floated the idea that men and women come from different planets. The science has moved us all on, as it so often does.) If I were to fall into Mars/Venus flytraps, however, I would say that the sensibility I need at the moment—from books, from life— is less likely to be found in books by men. I must apologize to the men who write perceptively, and with kindness and pity, about the overlooked corners of our emotional lives. I just haven't come across you recently. The book by a man I read and liked was a non-fiction book about Big Stuff.

There is divorce at the heart of both Priscilla Gilman's *The Critic's Daughter* and Emma Forrest's *Busy Being Free*— Gilman's parents, in the first, and Forrest's own, in the second. And both men involved had some kind of public life. Gilman's father was an influential drama critic; Forrest's husband was the Australian actor Ben Mendelsohn. Both books are resonant and very

Illustration by Kristian Hammerstad

particular, and they are both about love and its wrenching aftermath.

Gilman's book reminded me of how critics formed me. Now, I don't give much of a shit about many of them—who needs them when we have Rotten Tomatoes?—but when I was a teenager, I needed to be led by people I trusted toward things I would grow to love. I am almost sure I was the only person in my English suburban hometown who owned a hardback collection of Pauline Kael's reviews, and certainly the only teenager. I bought it from the remainder shelves of a Barnes & Noble on Fifth Avenue in New York City—and I read it, too, more than once. (*The Critic's Daughter*, however, reminds me that Kael wasn't always to be trusted. Gilman points out that she hated *West Side Story*, which is a little bit like—no, *exactly* like—hating life.) One of the reasons I loved Gilman's book is that through her father she makes a case for criticism as a worthwhile practice. If you've been on the receiving end of a kicking, as everyone in the arts has if they live long enough professionally, it's easy to forget that critics love the arts as much as their practitioners do. And it's easy to forget, too, that the best criticism can be as illuminating as any other form of writing. "That is what the highest criticism really is, the record of one's own soul," Oscar Wilde said, words that Gilman uses as an epigraph. My columns for *The Believer* might not be examples of "the highest criticism"—we rarely get above bungalow level here. But my soul has been bared for anyone to see, these last twenty years.

Richard Gilman was, among other things, the drama critic for *The Nation*, and after her parents' divorce, Priscilla was frequently by his side for first nights: hers was a childhood full of books, sports, musicals, authors, plays—a glorious upbringing, in many ways, were it not for her father crumbling after his divorce from her mother, a heavyweight literary agent. Priscilla discovered more about the marriage than was healthy for her—her father's affairs, his unsavory sexual predilections, his vulnerability, the dismally shaky foundations of the relationship. Her mother told her much of this, and her father confirmed some of it in his memoir, *Faith, Sex, Mystery*, published when Priscilla was in her teens. The book was panned by Francine Prose, praised by Mary Gordon, and if you need a cautionary tale about raising children when part of your life is available for public inspection, this is it. *The Critic's Daughter* is a book about a lot of things, but one of them is this: that a fierce and powerful voice, a voice that some people were afraid to hear, can disguise an awful lot of trouble and pain. The critic's daughter—the writer, as opposed to the book—has the tenderness, the acuity, and the facility to explore her father and her relationship to him in ways that cannot help but resonate. Maybe this is because all of us are the children of critics, in one way or another.

Emma Forrest's *Busy Being Free* is an extraordinarily frank account of her emotional and sexual life over the last few years, the Trump/COVID years, which in Forrest's case coincided with divorce and migration. Forrest has already written one beautiful, intense memoir, *Your Voice in My Head*, about another doomed relationship with a movie star, and Forrest's battle with mental illness; this book, like that one, is funny, compelling, and the product of a singular, valuable mind. Forrest's angular approach to her own material, as both a writer and a human, results in constant surprise: her response to Trump, for example, is a vow never to let anyone or anything penetrate her for

---

MICROINTERVIEW WITH WO CHAN, PART I

THE BELIEVER: Your debut collection is now out in the world, but I want to begin by casting back a few years. I remember you used to share poems as Facebook updates. They were so good, and I always thought, Why don't they have a book? I'm curious what that period of more informal circulation allowed.

WO CHAN: I haven't thought about my Facebook obsession for a while. That was a different time in my life; I was a different person. I liked that Facebook and social media gave me immediate validation, which isn't the deepest form of feedback, but it was what I needed at that moment. In that era, writers on Facebook were so supportive and you could have these wonderfully contained conversations. The format was also good for my attention span and specifically my capacity to hold pain, which is still pretty nonexistent, though I'm working on it. ✶

the duration of the presidency. "I didn't just give up sex—I gave up tampons and switched to period pants that are not only exterior but also *disgusting*—a Sheela-na-gig-level horror show."

Reading *Busy Being Free* isn't like reading at all, in the sense that you will never look at how many pages you have left, or wonder whether this was the page you got stuck on last night before sleep. It's more like drinking, or watching TV (no higher praise, in this books column). The confessions are sad, funny, brave, and horrifying: the divorce and period of celibacy that came afterward—and Harvey Weinstein—prompt a reevaluation of some of the sexual experiences she endured very early in her career. Every man should read *Busy Being Free*, I think, especially if said man is interested in any woman from a different generation. He may well end up self-Bobbitting, if he has half a brain or a quarter of a soul.

This brings us very neatly—another way of saying, *Aren't I clever?*—to Claire Dederer's *Monsters*, subtitled *A Fan's Dilemma*. You know exactly why those four words have been put together in that way, and the moment you see them, you think, Thank god! Someone is going to tell me what to do with Woody Allen and Roman Polanski. Who doesn't want to read this book? And, very quickly, you learn you are in safe hands. "I found I couldn't solve the problem of Roman Polanski by thinking," Dederer says in her introduction. And then, "The poet William Empson said life involves maintaining oneself between contradictions that can't be solved by analysis. I found myself in the midst of one of those contradictions." In other words, there is no answer. Of course there is no answer.

How could there be? I want to quote from just about every page of *Monsters*. First, because the idea that there is no answer is in itself both stimulating and liberating: it is not, after all, one's own stupidity (or masculinity, or questionable taste/moral judgment) that is preventing you from getting anywhere, despite your fears. And second, because this book is so damned smart: about films, books, art, and then, unexpectedly, about life.

There are all kinds of monsters in *Monsters*. The obvious suspects, yes, but also people you wouldn't necessarily have thought of: Joni Mitchell, who gave up a child for adoption; Doris Lessing, who left two children behind in South Africa to give herself a shot at international renown in London. Dederer is not saying these people are guilty of truly monstrous behavior—Polanski raped a child, after all, and how many artsy men have left children scattered all over the globe? But a woman's need to put her art before her children can result in the kind of

judgment reserved only for the most repugnant of men. Sometimes the art ends up beating out the monstrosity. What young bohemian woman hasn't, at one point, owned an image of Virginia Woolf, the anti-Semite and awful snob? Meanwhile Nabokov, the author of the most famous novel about a pedophile, is rescued here by a rather brilliant examination of the author's intentions, a critical approach that's in danger of going the same way as structuralism. There is a lot more to be said about *Monsters* than I can manage here, but I hope you take over, in your book groups, and with your friends; I can't think of a single person who wouldn't benefit from reading it. And, of course, it had to be written by a woman. You won't catch me writing about Polanski's greatness, or the hidden sympathy of *Lolita*. I have better things to do with my time than live in a bomb shelter.

I read *Tomorrow, and Tomorrow, and Tomorrow* on a personal recommendation, and it was the kind of recommendation that one simply can't ignore: firm, impassioned, delivered with some knowledge of the recommendee's tastes. I have aired my views on this before, but you know the worst kind of monster? The person who says, "I think you'd love it," within seconds of meeting you. Claire Dederer should write a whole book about those bastards. Ignorant recommendation is a much worse crime than abandoning your children. You can't look out a window without seeing a kid, whereas books you love are hard to find. Anyway, I wasn't surprised to discover that I loved Gabrielle Zevin's novel from the beginning.

The world of *TATAT*, as I suspect its fans will end up calling it, is the world of gaming. But to say it is a book about gaming is like saying that… you know what's coming next. I'm trying to stop myself, because it's a sentence I probably read once a month in a piece of arts journalism somewhere. OK: instead of referring to *Moby-Dick* and whales, I will try something different. To say it's a book about gaming is like saying that *Seinfeld* is a show about nothing, or that *War and Peace* is a book about war and peace… Oh, shit. It works, the *Moby-Dick* thing. Let's leave it alone for a while. What *TATAT* is really about is collaborative work and love, which is perhaps my favorite literary subgenre. It's very small, the subgenre, and I have only two other examples: Michael Chabon's *The Amazing Adventures of Kavalier and Clay* and Elizabeth McCracken's *Niagara Falls All Over Again*, two of my most cherished novels. *TATAT* belongs in that select group.

It's essentially a love triangle: there are two evidently brilliant games developers, Sam and Sadie, who have known each other since childhood, and a producer, Marx, who loves them both, although only one of them in the romantic sense. One reason novels about collaborative work are so winning is that they always involve success at some point in the journey; otherwise, nobody would bother writing about the collaboration. Most novels, it's fair to say, are not about success—not success that comes from the hearts and brains of likable protagonists, anyway. Sam, Sadie, and Marx achieve a great deal of success, and one of Zevin's triumphs is that she makes that success feel real, earned, and even, to a non-gamer, comprehensible: her love and understanding of the medium shine bright on every page. And toward the end, when life and success have done what they tend to do—namely, leave everyone in pieces—there is a long, beautiful chapter in which a game is populated by our heroes and their narratives, a breathtakingly chancy piece of writing that pays off in spades.

I hope you are not sick of me writing about Elizabeth Strout and her superlative novels. The trouble is, she keeps writing them, and I'm always going to read them, so here we are again. *Lucy by the Sea* is another Lucy Barton book; it's set during the pandemic, with Lucy and William, of *Oh William!* fame, moving out of New York City and up to Maine. Strout brings back the dread of those early weeks with more effectiveness than I was prepared for, and as a result the novel is more piercing than its predecessors, and they were sharp enough. If you haven't read any of them by now, then I'm wasting my time telling you about them.

As I write, Uruguay is playing South Korea in the World Cup on my TV in the other room. I'm not watching. It's more important to convince you to read great books by wonderful women writers. But if the referee can't see that Cavani was brought down inside the area just now, he needs his fucking eyes tested. ✶

ORIGINAL TITLES FOR CLASSIC NOVELS

✶ *The Last Man in Europe*, George Orwell's *1984*
✶ *The Kingdom by the Sea*, Vladimir Nabokov's *Lolita*
✶ *Fiesta*, Ernest Hemingway's *The Sun Also Rises*
✶ *The Year of the Rose*, Edith Wharton's *The House of Mirth*
✶ *All's Well That Ends Well*, Leo Tolstoy's *War and Peace*
✶ *Panasonic*, Don DeLillo's *White Noise*
✶ *Tomorrow Is Another Day*, Margaret Mitchell's *Gone with the Wind*
✶ *Under the Red, White, and Blue*, F. Scott Fitzgerald's *The Great Gatsby*
✶ *Second-Hand Lives*, Ayn Rand's *The Fountainhead*
✶ *Atticus*, Harper Lee's *To Kill a Mockingbird*
✶ *The War of the Rings*, J.R.R. Tolkien's *The Lord of the Rings*
✶ *The Mute*, Carson McCullers's *The Heart Is a Lonely Hunter*
✶ *Something That Happened*, John Steinbeck's *Of Mice and Men*
✶ *First Impressions*, Jane Austen's *Pride and Prejudice*
✶ *Alice*, Lewis Carroll's *Alice's Adventures in Wonderland*
✶ *Dark House*, William Faulkner's *Light in August*
✶ *Mistress Mary*, Frances Hodgson Burnett's *The Secret Garden*
✶ *Ulysses in Dublin*, James Joyce's *Dubliners*
✶ *Strangers from Within*, William Golding's *Lord of the Flies*

—List compiled by Eliza Browning

LOST ONES

EXPERTS AGREE THAT MEMORIES OF RARE MUSIC CAN PERSIST FOR MANY YEARS

by Ross Scarano

Decades later, Ben Ratliff, former pop music critic at *The New York Times*, can recall the details of a song he heard once, but that it is impossible for you to listen to. I'm sorry to report that it cannot be streamed. It cannot be purchased on a compact disc or a cassette, used or new. There's no rare vinyl pressing listed on Discogs. Ratliff's bit of recollected music criticism, shared over email, is a kind of ghost story.

My friend Laura Cantrell and I were in Nashville, her hometown. She talked our way into a Johnny Paycheck recording session, during a period after he'd shot someone and was appealing the charges. I think he was commercially dead because of the shooting incident. I was in awe of this homunculus, whose records I deeply loved, a terrible and charming person. On that day he seemed animated but tired—he'd clearly stayed up all the previous night. What were we doing there, college kids, unconnected nobodies? It was cool. I was sober as a judge but basically eye-pinned during this experience. These were the circumstances. I don't know what the recording session was for, but when he got out of the booth he entertained the engineers and the producers and us with a whole

stream of songs that I remember as harrowing. One was called "Looking Through the Eyes of a Dead Man." It was bright and up-tempo, like skiffle-tempo. Insane. A jaunty and almost jubilant song about death-in-life. That day he told me that it was to be part of an autobiographical record he was working on called "The Album of a Life." As far as I know he did not get to finish it. I asked him some years later if that song did indeed exist, at least in his head, if not on tape or on record, and he said it did. I can't find it online. He's long gone now.

When you work in the music industry, you often get to hear a piece of recorded music before it is filtered through the machine of a record label. At that time, before a marketing campaign has been deployed, the work is still subject to change. Sometimes you encounter a song that will not fade away, though you never hear it again. "Looking Through the Eyes of a Dead Man" may indeed live on magnetic tape in a box of studio detritus in a closet somewhere, but without Ratliff's story, there is nothing else to go by.

Speak with enough music journalists and these stories bubble up. Like the time Biggie didn't know how to get to the studio.

It's 1992, or thereabouts, and Christopher Wallace, newly signed to the

11

polished R&B label Uptown Records by Sean "Puff Daddy" Combs, is booked for his first real studio session for his debut album. He's a young man most accustomed to his neighborhood, Brooklyn's Clinton Hill, and truth be told he's super nervous about this appointment at Platinum Island, in downtown Manhattan. So he asks his friend and neighbor, an NYU film student and journalist named dream hampton, for directions. As Biggie is poised to make his mark on the world with his hyper-detailed storytelling and verbal style, hampton is on her way to becoming one of the greatest journalists to document hip-hop, writing with candor and care about Snoop Dogg, Tupac Shakur, and her friend Chris—soon to be world famous as the Notorious B.I.G.

She tells him: "Yo, you just take the C at Clinton–Washington, transfer at Jay Street to the F, take that to Broadway and whatchamacallit." Follow these instructions and then hoof it up the subway steps to eventually arrive at Platinum Island, at East Fourth and Broadway—easy. He tells her: "Nah, you coming with us." So hampton does, and hangs around while he works. Puffy has wisely put a more seasoned force in the studio with Big: Ol' Dirty Bastard, the Wu-Tang Clan's most irrepressible member, though at the time he goes by Ason.

Surrounded by the "attendant things" of the studio—the greenroom, the drinks and the weed, the "dorky white boy tech guy"—the duo records a song. "Ason was doing his pre-Drake singing bullshit and it was just great," hampton recollects over the phone. "He made Big feel so comfortable."

What they put to tape is ferocious and raw, and ultimately doesn't make it onto *Ready to Die*, the Notorious B.I.G.'s landmark saga of the everyday struggle in Rudy Giuliani's New York; doesn't become a bonus track on the anniversary edition; never finds its way onto any posthumous release. hampton doesn't know if it was ever mastered. While she talks, the song comes briefly alive. It is about as rare and special a song as can be, recorded by two legends dead long before they could be old.

There are a few ways to catch the song. Ratliff and hampton had their encounters off the clock, so to speak. In the industry there are on-assignment studio sessions where the writer shadows a musician for a story and gets a glimpse of something in progress that never leaves the windowless, soundproofed room of its creation. Insanul Ahmed, a writer who worked for Complex and Genius, can still hear a beat that Earl Sweatshirt played in 2012 at Mac Miller's home in Los Angeles, when Ahmed was profiling Miller. The late rapper had converted a small pool house into a recording studio that on any given night welcomed many of the region's most talented artists. Ahmed felt uneasy about this particular arrival because Earl had recently dissed Complex on a new single, "Chum." (He called out the staff, of which I was a member at that time, as "fuck n—.") "I don't know if he knows who I am," Ahmed thought—and he didn't exactly want him to find out. (Hostility toward the press is something of a tradition in music journalism, and Ahmed is no stranger to it, as evidenced by a well-publicized phone

confrontation between him and the rapper Wale.)

Earl sat down at the console and took over the room, playing music from what would become his debut album, *Doris*. Then he played beats of his own that he wanted to send to other artists. "I want to give this to André 3000," he said, queuing up a fresh selection. "It sounded like early morning in the jungle," Ahmed says. "Like, the sound of orangutans was part of the beat. It was crazy, with a really long build a full minute before it opened up. It was an art piece. I can still hear it in my head."

Some beats have a clearly defined pocket for an emcee to rhyme within, but this was inscrutable. "I don't know how someone would have rapped on it," Ahmed says, "though I guess André would have figured it out." There's little reason to doubt that he would have, André being André, but there's no record of it happening.

Outside the studio there are advance copies. In the heyday of print, before rampant piracy and filesharing on Napster, a cassette or CD would be shipped by the label to members of the press for coverage consideration. Mailed many months out from the release date in order to meet print deadlines, an early iteration of an album sometimes contained songs that wouldn't make the final cut, the result of further tinkering, or, in the case of many a hip-hop project, a sample-clearance issue. Nowadays, high-profile rap albums only rarely get shared in advance. If something unfinished circulates widely online, it's likely the result of someone hacking an artist's email.

Then there are listening sessions, where a label executive or publicist will summon a cadre of journalists to a nondescript carpeted conference room in Midtown Manhattan, where many labels and magazines have offices, or a cramped studio, to play the album closer to its release. Sometimes, the artist will travel to the publication's offices to play forthcoming music, and even though this occurs with regularity, it always—*always*—results in a screwball comedy of errors to get the speakers working. I shudder as I write this, reliving the interminable afternoon when the R&B singer Omarion and an entourage of a dozen watched mournfully as my colleagues and I flailed in our attempts to unlock the secrets of Bluetooth technology in real time.

Conversely, Naomi Zeichner, a writer and tech worker who served as editor in chief of *The FADER*, remembers the camaraderie these collisions between the press and an artist could inspire. Handlers and artists would stop by to present half-finished albums, looking for feedback on individual songs or the eventual sum of their parts. "They were there to play music, but also to pitch the narrative they hoped we'd be developing together as part of a long-lead magazine story," she says. "It was an opportunity to sniff each other out and build trust, or spot red flags."

In 2013, her favorite artist at the time, the Atlanta rapper and heart-on-his-sleeve balladeer Future, played an in-progress version of his sophomore album *Honest* for the magazine's staff. One track, a gem of brooding horniness called "Good Morning," imprinted on her in such a way that when a version of the song, with a similar melody

and different lyrics, appeared months later as the Beyoncé single "Drunk in Love," she felt as heartsick as she did proud. Both songs were produced by Detail and seemingly written around the same time, with the bigger star unsurprisingly winning rights to its release. (Future does not have a writing credit on Beyoncé's song.) "'Drunk in Love' is an incredible song," she says, "but it felt tragic that Future never released his version, which I thought proved his talent beautifully and which I had been waiting to hear again for months." "Good Morning" was never commercially released, but there are rips and performances of it online. A decade later, Future remains a chart topper, but the real heads will always wonder about the path not taken.

"There are tons of instances where I heard a song on the advance that didn't make it to the retail version," Joseph Patel explains over the phone. An Oscar and Grammy winner for coproducing the 2021 film *Summer of Soul*, Patel began his career writing about hip-hop and R&B for *Rap Pages, Paper,* and *Vibe* in the late '90s. That's how he heard the ur-version of Kanye West's "All Falls Down," with the Lauryn Hill sample, rather than the smoother Syleena Johnson interpolation; the first Clipse record, *Exclusive Audio Footage*, which included one Neptunes production that went to Jadakiss after the album was shelved by Elektra Records; and a very early draft of the N.E.R.D. debut, *In Search Of...*, which included two songs—"Why Must I Die" and "Here She Comes"— that never emerged anywhere else.

On YouTube, the site that I've come to think of as the most important music

library on the internet, I found "Guilty Girl," an excellent Puffy-produced Kelis song intended for her 2003 album, *Tasty*. Patel told me about it—the self-lacerating midtempo cut about wanting to cheat had stayed with him for almost twenty years, in part because he's from the Bay Area and the song used the same sample as "93 'til Infinity," the quintessential Northern California backpack rap track from Souls of Mischief. As of this writing, it's still available on YouTube, with fewer than five thousand views in the almost twelve years since it was posted. It sounds like a single to me, but at some point someone with power disagreed. "I'm about to make you hate me," Kelis sings on the hook, her sandpaper voice as pained as it is honest.

On YouTube, an upload like this is considered "user-generated content." Like a dubbed cassette, it's a pirated release that doesn't track back to a rights holder of the song; that is, it's not delivered to or claimed on the platform by a music rights holder— even though the song was technically funded with the coffers of no less a powerhouse than Sony Music, and the "users" behind the song's creation included Puff Daddy and the artist who sang the hook on "Got Your Money." There's no telling how it moved from the studio to the anonymous account that uploaded it.

YouTube even hosts a portion of the song that the Notorious B.I.G. and Ol' Dirty Bastard recorded that day at Platinum Island (with dream hampton in attendance), though it's incomplete, cutting off the second verse from Biggie after a handful of bars. It is an abridged document of a momentous day in music history, and it's also something of a false start. The verses you can hear on this upload appear in their complete form on two solo songs from Big and ODB: "Gimme the Loot" and "Brooklyn Zoo," respectively. Those finished songs sound better than what you hear on the leaked excerpt.

I would love the opportunity to test my memory of my lost song, my grail, to know if it's as good as I remember. In early 2015 I went to a Manhattan listening party for a forthcoming release from The-Dream, one of the architects of contemporary R&B and a personal favorite. I went with my friend and colleague Damien Scott, also a devotee. With catering from Miss Lily's and a trim guest list, this wasn't representative: typically you're shoulder to shoulder in the studio sipping tepid Cîroc from a plastic cup; the volume for the looped advance single is deafening; and when the album playback begins, there's only the performance of listening amid rampant picture snapping and networking.

This night was different. After the requisite milling around and greeting the writers, podcast hosts, and publicists, The-Dream introduced *Crown*, a concise return to form after the lackluster *IV Play*, the first shaky release in a career that was otherwise stunning for its ingenuity and ambition.

When the project finished playing, Damien asked if they would run back a song called "Cedes Benz." I didn't know you could make a request like that. I was years into my career and I still hadn't tested enough of the limits. Rooms like that could bring out

a capacity for ingratiation in myself that I didn't like. Outside the office, at the label or at a show or in the studio, I wanted to sink into the furniture or blend into the walls rather than stand out. When Damien asked, it was obvious how well the move worked as flattery—his request excited The-Dream. But he hadn't meant it as a move. He really wanted to hear it one more time. This is why I've heard twice the best song I'll never hear again.

There's currently a version of "Cedes Benz" available to stream, but it isn't what I heard The-Dream play that night in 2015. For over three minutes, I listened, stunned, as he broke into a pulverizing near-rap cadence about the splendor of German engineering and the power of driving a car so clean it makes your rivals sick. The production skitters and grinds, replicating the commotion and noise of combustion underneath the hood. Then he brings in his girl, who looks so good it renders irrelevant the car he's hyped up. She's so bad that "these

bitches hate it when they see her. / Bet you thought you was a diva, and she should apologize: Baker, Anita." The beat falls out and something sleek glides in, built from the velvet bones of Anita Baker's 1994 hit single "I Apologize." The-Dream duets with Baker as she sings with heartrending contrition. At once airy and deep, her voice is a feather capable of knocking you backward. And the way her strong alto pairs with The-Dream's boyish upper range is nothing less than fantastical. The unexpected joy of these voices brought together created an illusion so beautiful I wanted to live in it.

That's how I remember it, anyway. We ate banana pudding afterward.

Listening to the song now is a tease: the door in time created by the mention of Baker's name never opens for her to step through. She's summoned, but the sample doesn't arrive. She wouldn't clear the rights to use it; he recorded a new piece of music that feels indebted to her without using any of her music. It's merely good instead of miraculous.

I tried to hear the song again but had no luck. Even The-Dream's engineer turned me down, saying the song wasn't his to share. I get it. When I explained my predicament to Ratliff, he gave me the linguistic equivalent of a smack upside the head: "You're asking about recorded music, but I can't help thinking that's a very small part of what a 'song' is," he wrote. The power of the impermanent music experience is "more than a matter of recordable and copyrightable sound. I *love* being told, 'Sorry, fucker, you will never hear this again.' Let the great thing have its ungovernable value." ✦

LOVE AND DEATH SPEAKING AT ONCE

A NEW POEM

by Emily Jungmin Yoon

We come together.
To love someone means to imagine their death.

2 a.m. and you lie awake in fear of us. *What if?*
What if? Call your mother. Say you're sorry.

Call your father. What? Call your sister. Memory sustains,
memory fades. Take a picture. Keep a journal. Underline,

doggy-ear, leave margin-notes in your book, mark it
with your touch. Do not go into a mountain alone.

Write the letter that embarrasses you: the most adulating,
undulating language, each line a petal in a dahlia.

Fields of swaying dahlias, you make them.
Yes, you can. Give that person a bouquet of dahlias,

grown, then cut for you; that is us, together. If we make in you
such tender-hearted anticipation—is it so bad, us together?

FAME FOR FAME

by Noah Van Sciver

UNDERWAY

WE ASK WRITERS AND ARTISTS: WHAT'S ON YOUR DESK? WHAT ARE YOU WORKING ON?

by Danielle A. Jackson

Issues of Oxford American
I always have the most recent issues on hand. We hold a number of meetings throughout the week and are constantly brainstorming new ideas and referring back to what we've already done.

Book stack
I am always reading for my day job, school, or my writing, and sometimes for pleasure. Dilla Time by Dan Charnas was the last book I read just for myself.

Logitech MK295 Wireless Keyboard
I have a hybrid setup with an Apple desktop and a PC keyboard that sometimes poses a problem for shortcuts in InDesign. I used to be a middle manager at an advertising firm, and the all-PC habits I learned there die hard.

To-Do List
My to-do list necessarily includes tasks from all my various gigs. Notice: paying contributors is at the top of my list!

Crystals
The writer Harmony Holiday told me rose quartz was a "gentle stone," and I aim for a spirit of gentleness, even through obstacles.

Aretha Franklin
One of several photographs of important artists around me, this image of Franklin reminds me to keep going, and to experiment. Over seventy-six years, Aretha sang a little bit of everything.

Currently I'm working on a longform essay about a Black film that tackles the effects of gentrification for Criterion. For a longer nonfiction project, I'm writing about women, movement, and the Great Migration out of the South. More than half the migrants who left for cities in the North, the Midwest, and the West were girls and women. They moved for better work, or school, or love, or bodily autonomy. My entry into these ideas is through the journeys of the women in my family. My great-grandmother was born enslaved just outside Selma, Alabama. She moved west, to northern Mississippi; her youngest daughter moved north to Chicago and to Memphis, Tennessee, and opened a hybrid restaurant and juke, where the food and music she served nurtured other exiles from the countryside. Her youngest daughter gave birth to me in Memphis. Our lives stretch across the whole of the twentieth century. By intermingling family stories and archival study, I'm hoping to tell a history of the lasting cultural influence of the Mississippi Delta. ✷

18

Illustration by Kristian Hammerstad

ASK CARRIE

A QUARTERLY COLUMN FROM
CARRIE BROWNSTEIN, WHO IS BETTER
AT DISPENSING ADVICE THAN TAKING IT

Send questions to advice@thebeliever.net

Q: *A couple weeks ago, my boyfriend told me for the first time that he loved me—in French. He's not from France and doesn't speak the language, but even now when I say it, his response is always "Je t'aime." He says it like it's this joke between us, but I still wonder if something is holding him back from saying it in English. Can I really trust that he loves me?*

Pourquoi?, Boston, MA

A: On first blush, there's something romantic about being loved only in a foreign language, as if love were a destination, a private island. The strange words beckon; you grab your passport and leave the ordinary behind.

Yet I can't help but think of the deception and confusion lurking behind this fantasy. You're not being transported; you're being marooned. Because your boyfriend isn't a native French speaker, what he's presenting seems more illusion than reality. What you're being asked to translate are not the words themselves but whether he's ascribing any meaning to them. Does "Je t'aime" mean that he loves you or that he doesn't? It's so close to the actual thing, but it's an impostor, an uncanny valley of affection.

So I think you are right to be concerned. Replace "He says he loves me only in French" with "He says he loves me only when he's drunk" or "He says he loves me only via text message," and the issue becomes a lot clearer.

If you're tired of your relationship feeling like a transaction in a foreign currency (thank you, Deborah Eisenberg), you need to ask him how he really feels. Because while he thinks saying "I love you" in French is a joke the two of you share, it sounds more like a painful disparity. Honesty is not unique to any one language, and words are often nothing more than words. But no matter which ones your boyfriend uses, whether foreign or familiar, make sure you believe him.

If it doesn't work out, I highly recommend a trip to France.

Q: *I remember being a kid and hating how grown-ups always commented on my changed height, and how they said they remembered when I was yea tall, et cetera. But now I find myself extremely self-conscious when I meet someone under age sixteen and fall back on these comments. Any suggestions for some conversation starters?*
Amber S.
Tucson, AZ

A: Your question comes at a time when I've been grappling with this very subject. At social events, I've noticed myself playing friend matchmaker for my partner's daughter, based on a single broad

Illustration by Kristian Hammerstad

criterion: her age. As in "Hi, Oliver. Nice to see you! This is Margo. She's also ten." Then, when Margo isn't keen to immediately go off and play with Oliver, I'm flummoxed: Wouldn't Margo rather hang out with another kid than with me? Apparently not. Or maybe Margo doesn't want to hang out with her elders and also doesn't want to fraternize with a stranger based on the fact that they were born the same year. After a few of these failed friend setups, it dawned on me how absolutely ridiculous it is to assume like-mindedness or compatibility based on an arbitrary number. Imagine saying to an adult, *Tom, have you met Greg? He's also forty-one!*, and then waiting for them to go off and make a crayon drawing together. Amber, my point is, a lot of us grown-ups are guilty of these reductive, unimaginative behaviors toward kids.

While our intentions are benevolent, these actions seem like a narrowing and misunderstanding of childhood existence, one that we should know—because we've been there—is both complex and dynamic. So my advice to you is also what I've been telling myself: treat kids with the same respect and decorum you'd use with adults.

Here, too, is an opportunity to have sympathy for the adults who fumbled their way through interactions with us in our youth. When one of my parents' friends saw me with a botched spiral perm and braces, confidently talking about how New Kids on the Block were better than the Beatles, I can only imagine that remarking on my height was not merely the safest but the only option.

Yet I think we can improve on how we were treated as youngsters, or at least try. I find that asking questions is the best way to engage with kids. Even if their answers are monotone and monosyllabic, at least you've given them an opening to share and converse. (You'll know soon enough whether it's worth continuing or if the very sight of you is cringeworthy, a rejection that will send you into a spiral ending with a pseudo-clothing purchase from a semi-legitimate company that targeted you on Instagram.) Content-wise, I'd avoid the following subjects unless prompted: TikTok, K-pop, Hyperpop, SoundCloud rappers, Sabrina Carpenter, crop tops, pajama bottoms as legitimate going-out pants, and gaming. Mentioning that you once played *Beat Saber* on a VR headset might suggest joie de vivre on your dating app profile, but it's not going to move the needle with the under-sixteen crowd.

Last, if all else fails and you want to ensure you're treating everyone equally—adults and kids alike—might

I suggest telling your grown-up friends how short they're getting?

Q: *Should I force my dog to walk in the rain? I don't want to make her do something she doesn't want to do, but I also know it's good for her. Please help!*
Sula
Toronto, ON

A: In short, yes. Dogs of all shapes, ages, and sizes can and will survive a walk in the rain. Exercise and mental stimulation are crucial for a dog's well-being, and, though it's the most cliché saying in the dog training world, "a tired dog is a good dog." But it's true! Lots of mild behavioral issues—excessive chewing, barking, digging, et cetera—are due to boredom and lack of exercise. So you're right: a walk is good for your pup, rain or shine.

My two dogs and I live in the Pacific Northwest, so pups in this part of the world are out of luck if they don't like the rain. That said, there are plenty of dogs I know who look like they're auditioning for those Sarah McLachlan ASPCA commercials every time water grazes their fur. *Help me!* they seem to say. And by *help* they mean, *Book me a flight to California. Also, I only fly private.*

Given your dog's aversion to the rain, one of two things is likely occurring, or maybe a bit of both. First, you might have unwittingly "captured" a behavior you didn't want. Perhaps one rainy day, your dog made a cute, forlorn face and tucked her tail when you tried to take her out, so you bent down to pet and comfort her. Or she refused to walk, so you took her back home, where she cuddled up next to you on the couch. What your dog learned is that when it's raining, if she comports herself in a certain way, she's rewarded in the form of attention and affection. Now she's more likely to continue those behaviors because she likes what she gets in return. Second, for whatever reason, your dog may truly dislike the rain. In either case, the goal is for your dog to develop positive associations with the rain.

The first thing I'd do is buy a high-value treat that she gets only on rainy-day walks. Do not give her this treat in the house or on any other occasion. But the second she steps outdoors and into the rain… ta-da! She gets a treat. You may have to lure her at first. The key to this exercise is staying neutral or ignoring her when she refuses to come along. You may have to momentarily step outside alone and shut the door behind you. Remember, you're also a reward for your dog, and by leaving without her, you're removing something she likes. Then calmly open the door and try luring her again, treating or giving verbal praise only with forward movement. If she still refuses to go, you might head back inside and ignore her for five minutes. Just go about your business, no eye contact, no petting. Then try again. As you get closer to the door and she follows, return your attention to her and verbally praise her. If she follows you out the door this time, give her those treats and even more verbal praise. Soon enough, your dog will realize that going outside in the rain is full of positive things: attention, affection, and treats!

Once you're outside, praise her often, be encouraging, and keep the high-value treats on hand in case you need to administer them for the first couple of blocks. Then make the walk fun and incorporate training to distract her from the rain and put her brain in work mode. Ask her to sit at street corners and give her a treat. If she knows other commands, like "Watch me" or "Shake," have her practice those, too, and give her treats accordingly. Once the dog is on her way, she'll likely stop caring about the terrible weather. Hopefully after a few of these sessions, your dog will forget any negative associations with the rain, you can give treats less often, and the reward will be the walk itself and spending time with you.

And, fine, if you want, get her a cute raincoat! ✶

RELIGIONS CREATED BY ANTHROPOMORPHIC ANIMALS IN NOVELS

✶ El-ahrairah (rabbits), *Watership Down*
  by Richard Adams
✶ The Queen (bees), *The Bees* by Laline Paull
✶ Herne (deer), *Fire Bringer* by David Clement-Davies
✶ Another (deer), *Bambi, A Life in the Woods*
  by Felix Salten
✶ Sita (wolves), *The Sight* by David Clement-Davies
✶ The Wind/Pan (wild animals), *The Wind in the Willows*
  by Kenneth Grahame
✶ Animalism (farm animals), *Animal Farm*
  by George Orwell
✶ The Uplifted (rats), *Mrs. Frisby and the Rats of NIMH* by Robert C. O'Brien
✶ Meerclar Allmother (cats), *Tailchaser's Song*
  by Tad Williams
✶ The Stone (moles), *Duncton Wood*
  by William Horwood
✶ The Fingers (ants), *Empire of the Ants*
  by Bernard Werber
✶ The Heavenly Horse (horses), *The Heavenly Horse from the Outermost West*
  by Mary Stanton
✶ Nocturna (bats), *Silverwing* by Kenneth Oppel
✶ Lord Man (cockroaches), *The Cockroaches of Stay More*
  by Donald Harington
✶ Racing (dogs), *The Art of Racing in the Rain*
  by Garth Stein

—list compiled by Emily Lang

SACRIFICE ZONE

A SEMI-REGULAR GUEST COLUMN
ABOUT REGULARLY IGNORED PLACES.
IN THIS ISSUE: LAND'S END, UK

by Meara Sharma

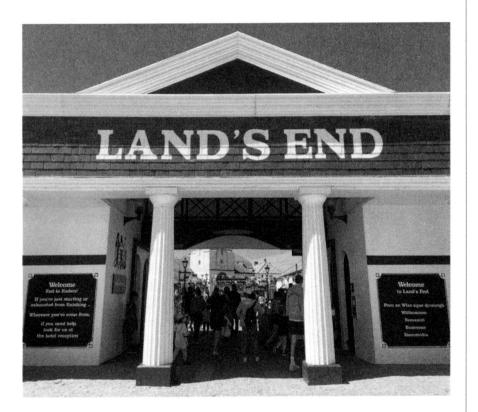

When you arrive at Land's End, there's no mistaking where you are, and yet you cannot see it. What you can see—at this southwesternmost tip of England, this cliff-edge of Britannia, where the Cornwall peninsula claws into the Celtic Sea—is a parking lot. Then you can see the words LAND'S END emblazoned on an enormous Doric-columned entrance, the width of a four-lane highway, beside which the open-topped Land's End Coaster deposits busloads of tourists. Then you can see Land's End doughnuts, and Land's End ice cream, and the boots of a man who walked naked from Land's End to the north tip of Great Britain. You can see Land's End

Photos by the author

  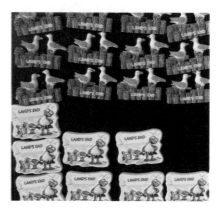

teddy bears, and Land's End stuffed octopuses, and Land's End pillows shaped like giant Cornish pasties, the famous thick-crusted savory tarts once meant for miners to eat underground and now among the region's biggest exports.

You can see an immersive journey into the legend of King Arthur, replete with fire-breathing dragons and the "latest interactive technology." And a "4D Film Experience," in which you plot your escape from a ship of swashbuckling pirates. And you can see families waiting in line to be photographed beneath the "iconic" LAND'S END signpost, which indicates that New York City is 3,147 miles away, and which has a customizable slot for your name and the distance you are from your own hometown (THE BLANDFORDS, BROADBOTTOM: 344 MILES).

So what is it you cannot see? In this place that bellows its name from every direction, it is easy to forget where you are. Behind the souvenirs and the cinemas, the fast food and the flashing lights, that which actually surrounds you—windswept headlands, weather-sculpted cliffs rising high above wild waves, razorbills and sea campion and basking sharks—has been disciplined into a backdrop.

This other Land's End is hidden in the strata of its 270-million-year-old granite cliffs, in the shifting edges of its shoreline. It's a place that for millennia has stirred, with its raw beauty, its epic position, a deep sense of the sublime: that exalted, terrifying greatness ("mingled with Horrours, and sometimes almost with despair," wrote John Dennis). The ancient Greeks deemed it Belerion—the place of the sun—and in its shining aura, Bronze Age peoples laid sacred stone circles and buried their dead. When its Cornish name, Penwith Steort, meaning "extreme end," came into use in 997 CE, it captured the spiritual potency of a place at the outermost reaches, with its ragged border between land and sea, known and unknown. Crossing such a boundary, in Celtic mythology, is a way into the Otherworld. After the end, a beginning. As poet Henry Alford characterized these cliffs in 1860: "Look out upon the glorious realms of hope, / And find the last of earth,—the first of God."

This Land's End—of poetry, of worship, of extra-human sublimity—is hard to find, smothered as it is by tourist paraphernalia, a shopping mall at the end of the world. The man-made version of Land's End, while trying to fulfill a consumerist notion of what befits such an endpoint, ignores the soul of the place, that which drew us to it to begin with. In a sense, it's the inverse of László Krasznahorkai's story of a man who goes to the Acropolis but is unable to see this wonder of Western civilization for what it is, because he's completely blinded by the summer sun. "He was never even going to see the Acropolis, even though he was here at the Acropolis," he laments. In the natural wonder that is Land's End, it is our own human-made materialism that blinds us to it.

This is, of course, a phenomenon of our time, the self-destructive compulsion to shut our eyes and drain the earth for our fleeting desires (pipelines in old-growth forests, mountains bombed for bauxite, et cetera, et cetera). But in Land's End, a place whose very name conjures something beyond comprehension, something greater than us, there is a crystalline object lesson in the cognitive dissonance between what we've made and what we're obscuring—what we need to retrieve. ✲

CLOSE READ

UNPACKING ONE REDOUBTABLE PASSAGE.
IN THIS ISSUE: AN EXCERPT FROM
THE EXPERIENCE OF LANDSCAPE BY JAY APPLETON

by Molly Young

Appleton proposes that we instinctively grade landscapes based on how "survivable" they are. When a landscape strikes your eyes and brain as a place where you could hypothetically thrive, you convert this intuition into an aesthetic evaluation: "What a gorgeous painting!" or "I love what you've done with your stately grounds! This is what Appleton calls "habitat theory."

Nested within "habitat theory" is a contingent theory called "prospect-refuge theory." (Don't panic, there are no additional theories.)

When postulate *rears its head, you know we're dealing with an academic text. This slightly arid excerpt comes from a 1975 book,* The Experience of Landscape, *by the British geographer and poet Jay Appleton. Perhaps we can sprinkle a little bit of water on it in the form of annotations...*

Habitat theory postulates that aesthetic pleasure in landscape derives from the observer experiencing an environment favourable to the satisfaction of his biological needs. Prospect-refuge theory postulates that, because the ability to see without being seen is an intermediate step in the satisfaction of many of those needs, the capacity of an environment to ensure the achievement of this becomes a more immediate source of aesthetic satisfaction.

The Experience of Landscape is neither geography nor poetry but it is loosely informed by both. I'd characterize it as a charming alloy of aesthetic theory and Professor Appleton's Shower Thoughts.

Appleton begins his book with a question: "What do we like about landscape and why do we like it?" He's talking about "landscape" in life, but also in art: gardens, vistas, paintings, photographs... even descriptions of scenery in poems.

Combine a prospect with a refuge and you hit the survivability jackpot: a place where you can see without yourself being seen. In other words, a place with offensive advantages (you can scan for prey) and defensive advantages (you can hide from predators). In other-other words, "a room with a view."

A ROOM WITH A VIEW
E. M. Forster

In the book's conclusion, Appleton suggests that habitat theory is "a bridge passage played on a solo instrument... not very important, perhaps, in itself, but leading the imagination onwards into the next movement, in which the full orchestra must be involved." Here we must applaud his modesty. Wouldn't you love to end every email you write— every conversation you undertake—with a similar disclaimer? (Really, what's stopping you?)

Appleton analyzes landscapes in terms of "features" and "situations." These include caves, ravines, forests, panoramas, fog, mountains, rocks, individual trees, and clumps of reeds. You might think, Hold on. What is the difference between a "feature" and a "situation"? Isn't a cave both of those things? And indeed, Appleton was faulted in contemporaneous reviews for a certain fuzziness.

However. A non-fuzzy element is his idea that humans love features and situations that allow us a wide view of our surroundings, like a mountaintop or a climbable tree. In Appleton's terminology, these are "prospects."

We also cherish features and situations that allow us to hide, such as a well-positioned boulder or a clump of reeds. These he calls "refuges."

See figure A. Landscapes that feature a balance of prospects and refuges—and perhaps even two-in-one specials— are, Appleton says, the most beautiful landscapes of all.

Figure A

PROSPECT: *Hilltop for gazing*

REFUGE: *Clump of bushes in which to lurk*

FLAVOR FLAV

[HYPEMAN]

"TO ALL THE PEOPLE THAT'S DEAD: COME ALIVE."

Dishes Flavor Flav learned to cook at his family's diner in Freeport, Long Island:
Fried chicken
Mashed potatoes
Mac and cheese
Greens (and also lima beans)

The role of a hip-hop hypeman is to take an audience—whether bored or eager, sleepy or anxious—and transform them into a cohesive, screaming crowd, ready to dance and hungry for a good time. No one fills that role quite like Flavor Flav.

William Drayton Jr. was born in Long Island in 1959, and rose to fame in the late '80s as Flavor Flav, the legendary hypeman of Public Enemy, the group that gave rap a political edge with its debut, Yo! Bum Rush the Show. Serving as a comedic foil to the stern front man Chuck D, Flav blazed a path across the stage like a pied piper of hip-hop, urging people to get out of their seats, follow along with the song, and turn up for a party. When he wasn't pumping up the crowd, Flav would take the mic on songs like "Too Much Posse," "911 Is a Joke," and "Cold Lampin' with Flavor."

Illustration by Kristian Hammerstad

His charismatic stage presence and his unique ability to accessorize—transforming a large clock from a strange timepiece into statement jewelry—gave Flav his own fan base. He earned even more fans when he reinvented himself in the 2000s on VH1's reality series The Surreal Life, *where he shacked up with the legendary Charo, New Kid on the Block Jordan Knight,* Full House *star Dave Coulier, and model and actress Brigitte Nielsen for our viewing pleasure. That was followed by a romantic spin-off series with Nielsen called* Strange Love, *and then his own reality dating show,* Flavor of Love, *which lasted three seasons.*

Now, at age sixty-four, Flav is two-years-and-counting sober. He's back to making music and looking toward the future, while nodding to the past. When August 2023 rolls around, it will be the fiftieth anniversary of the birth of hip-hop, marking the day when eighteen-year-old DJ Kool Herc changed music forever. While Herc started the party, it's hard to imagine hip-hop without its biggest hypeman, Flavor Flav.

—Melissa Locker

I. THE OWNER OF NEW YORK

THE BELIEVER: Where in the world are you?

FLAVOR FLAV: Right now I'm in Manhattan. I am in New York City, in the streets of New York.

BLVR: Do you feel like you own the town?

FF: Sure do. And I'm gonna own it for the rest of my life, until the day I die. Even though I live in Vegas, I still own New York.

BLVR: Is there a song that goes through your head when you're in New York?

FF: There's no songs that come into my head about New York when I come to New York outside of "Empire State of Mind." That's what I'm talking about! Jay Z and Alicia Keys. And Frank Sinatra—old blue eyes. "It's up to you, New York, New York." That's what plays through my mind too.

BLVR: You were born and raised on Long Island, right?

FF: Yeah. I was born in Freeport. Born and raised in Freeport. I moved to Roosevelt [Long Island] when I was fourteen. I finished growing up there. And I have a fun fact: when I moved to Roosevelt in 1974, Eddie Murphy was in my ninth-grade English class.

BLVR: Really? Eddie Murphy, Eddie Murphy?

FF: Yes, we had a teacher named Mrs. Muckle. I'll never forget it, man. But, yep, that's part of my bragging rights.

BLVR: Between you and Eddie Murphy, who was the class clown? Who was in trouble more often?

FF: I was the class clown *and* I was in trouble more. Eddie wasn't a class clown around that time.

BLVR: It took him a while to achieve that status?

FF: Probably once he became a teenager and all that.

BLVR: What was the most trouble you got into in that class?

FF: I didn't stay in the Roosevelt High School long. I got kicked out and put back in Freeport High School.

BLVR: Oh no. Was it because of Mrs. Muckle?

FF: No, it wasn't because of Mrs. Muckle. It was because I was the Dennis the Menace of the society. Not just of the school, but of the society. I ain't gonna lie, I was a very mischievous kid.

But that's all just part of growing up and stuff and, you know, peer pressure. Sometimes you hang out with the wrong crowd because you want to be the talk of the town. You want to be the man, you want to be the—the one everybody's talking about. I was more of a follower than a leader, but yet I still was a leader, because I did have people following me.

BLVR: Do you think you've changed much since you were a kid?

FF: Around that time, I was fourteen, fifteen. Today, I'm sixty-three. So what do you think?

BLVR: So, yeah, I'm going to guess you've changed?

FF: People do change with time. But there are certain things within people that don't change. You know what I'm saying? And, you know, that's genuine.

BLVR: That's very true. I mean, look at Eddie Murphy. He went from being just a normal kid in your class to suddenly being one of the most famous comedians around.

FF: He sure did. And I am so proud of my man. Very proud of him and his come-up. I do miss his brother, Charlie, who was one of my good friends.

BLVR: Charlie Murphy did *True Hollywood Stories*, right?

FF: Yeah, I think he did. There was a lot of stuff that Charlie did touch that I don't really know about too much. But I know Charlie was out there. Charlie had himself out there doing his thing before he passed away. Yeah, man, that was my boy. Man, I really miss him.

BLVR: Did he go to high school with you as well?

FF: He did. I mean, they were both in school around the time that I got to Roosevelt: both of them were there.

BLVR: This high school seems to have put out a lot of incredibly famous people. Do any of you get invited back to speak?

FF: I've been back to speak on a couple of occasions. The reason is because I love giving back to where I come from. It's only right that you do, you know what I'm saying? That's my roots, you know? I don't care how big of a tree you get to be, one day you're gonna have to go back to your roots for something. That's true.

II. A NATURAL CAREER

BLVR: Speaking of roots, you're in New York, you're staying in Manhattan, but you grew up in Long Island. Do you feel like Long Island needs a hypeman?

FF: You mean does Long Island need *another* hypeman? The reason I say that is because you know I'm the first, the original hypeman.

BLVR: Yes, of course. All due respect to the original hypeman!

But do you think Long Island needs someone to build it up a little bit?

FF: Even though I did move out of New York State, I don't feel that Long Island lost its hypeman. I feel that Long Island is always gonna have its hypeman. As long as I live, as long as I breathe air, you know? Even though I don't live there, it always represents home.

BLVR: So if, say, the New York Tourism Board came to you and said, *We need people to go to Long Island. Can you hype it up in the press?*, what would be your sales pitch?

FF: Check this out. My sales pitch would be: *To all the people that's dead: come alive. No jive. Let's strip and strive.* That's my sales pitch.

BLVR: That's a good one! I now feel like I need to go to Long Island.

FF: No doubt, no doubt.

BLVR: That said, have you heard of the Montauk Monster?

FF: No.

BLVR: There was a mysterious creature that washed up on the shores of Long Island.

FF: Oh boy. Is this another one of those Bigfoot stories, Loch Ness monster stories?

BLVR: It is! I mean, it's not as scary as Long Island traffic, but it's still pretty scary.

FF: I never heard of that before. That's a brand-new one to me.

BLVR: Yeah, I'm going to look up details for you right now, because I feel like we need to discuss this.

FF: We need to discuss the monster? Why do I need to discuss the monster? To make friends with him? Or are you trying to get me to be the monster's hypeman?

BLVR: Absolutely! If you're going to be Long Island's hypeman, you're going to have to hype for the monster too.

FF: I need to know exactly about the monster, huh, Melissa?

BLVR: For sure, you need to know what you're going to be facing. Oh look, discoverlongisland.com says there's a Long Island Monster Gallery.

FF: There's a Long Island Monster Gallery out there? Where is it located?

BLVR: It's in Mineola.

FF: Are you serious? That's crazy. I thought I knew all about Mineola.

BLVR: So you really haven't heard of the Montauk Monster?

FF: No, I haven't heard of any of these monsters.

BLVR: It was an animal carcass that washed ashore in Montauk in 2008. But no one could ever figure out what type of animal it was.

FF: Did they figure out what the animal was? Did they get a picture of it?

MICROINTERVIEW
WITH WO CHAN, PART II

THE BELIEVER: I have always admired your drag, and wonder how performing in drag has brought about today's Wo Chan.

WO CHAN: I think my drag offers a similar comfort to writing online, actually. If you're a drag queen, when you get onstage, there is an understanding among queer people that the audience will validate you. They support you for getting onstage and being brave. Even if you're having a bad day performing. ✶

BLVR: They do have a lot of pictures of it. It's not attractive. You're the professional, but it might be hard to hype up.

FF: I would love to see it. I would love to see what a monster looks like. To see the monster in real life. I mean, you know, I've seen them on TV and dreamed about them.

BLVR: You dream about monsters?

FF: When you're a kid you always dream about monsters and shit. One time when I was little, I had a dream that Godzilla and I became the best of friends. That was my boy! Just like King Kong.

BLVR: I love that! It's very optimistic that, like, you and Godzilla would meet and be friends. It shows good self-confidence. Do you feel like you had a lot of self-confidence as a kid?

FF: I sure did. That's why I am who I am right now. I couldn't have been who I am right now without confidence.

BLVR: Where do you think that confidence came from?

FF: From God. From him: he gave me the notion to know that I can do certain things in life. I had confidence in myself that I could do these things, you know? So that's where I say my confidence comes from, really. I'm saying it comes from God. It's a personal feeling from God.

BLVR: And that confidence helped you become a hypeman. How did that start?

FF: Well, that came from being at parties, being on the microphone, getting everybody to get up out of their seats and on the floor at the party. And I just brought that into rap music. So when we'd be on the stage, I'd be telling everybody, *Come on, get out of your seat! Come on, everybody, raise your hands in the air. Everybody say, "Oho!"* You know, all that is hyping up the crowd.

BLVR: And then it became your career.

FF: And you know what? It became my career without me even trying to do it. It just naturally happened.

BLVR: That's amazing. Most people would love a career to just happen to them. What is your definition of a hypeman's job?

FF: My definition of a hypeman's job is to hype up the crowd when the crowd is dead.

BLVR: Have you ever found it impossible to hype up a crowd?

FF: No, never. I've always found that to be possible. And I was always the type of person who was like, *Hey, look, listen, man. If you don't want to get your dead ass out of the seat, stay there and be dead! Fuck it! I know one thing: we're gonna be hype without you.* So that's my attitude to people that don't want to be hype.

III. THE SOUL/SOLE DINER

BLVR: Did you ever think about being anything other than a hypeman?

FF: Just a musician and that's about it. I always wanted to be famous through music, like Herbie Hancock, Stanley Clarke, and James Brown. So I became famous through music; it's just that I came from a different part of the ball field. I got famous, but as they say, be careful what you ask for, because you just might get it. I asked for this. And I got it.

BLVR: Do you regret it at all?

FF: Nah, man. God is good, man. I don't regret the gifts that God gives me.

BLVR: Do you ever find fame challenging? It seems so double-edged, great in certain ways, but also you can't just go out for some soup without being surrounded by people.

FF: Yeah, it happens. It comes with the territory. I ain't gonna lie, but I feel like I handle it very well.

BLVR: Have you had a particularly memorable fan interaction?

FF: One of my most favorite fan interactions was me hugging this lady because she seen me and she started crying, but with happiness. It was through tears of happiness. She couldn't believe that she was seeing Flavor Flav. And I was like one of her most favorite people in the world. And this lady could not stop crying for nothing! And I went over and I hugged her and tried to console her and tell her, "Hey, look, listen, ma'am, it's OK. It's all right." But this lady would not stop bawling for nothing! I felt so good inside because she was crying about me. It could have been crying about anybody else in the world, but it ended up being Flavor Flav!

BLVR: That's sweet, but I think I would be alarmed if someone burst into tears when they saw me.

FF: Well, I was a little concerned for a second, like, *Dammit, lady, am I ugly? Why the fuck are you crying? Does my breath stink?* But it was tears of happiness. It was tears of joy.

BLVR: I know you've always wanted to be famous for music, but I also hear you're pretty famous for your cooking. When did you start cooking?

FF: I started cooking when I was young. I used to always watch my mom and my aunts make prepared dinners and stuff like that. My mother and my dad ended up owning a restaurant, and that's when I really learned how to cook: inside our restaurant. It was called the Soul Diner in Freeport, Long Island. That's when I really learned how to really, really cook my lima beans and my rice and fried chicken and greens, mashed potatoes, mac and cheese, all kinds of stuff.

BLVR: I hear your fried chicken is better than Wolfgang Puck's.

FF: For me it is! But one day, me and Wolfgang are going to do a chicken standoff and the loser has to jump into the swan pond at the Hotel Bel-Air. The restaurant inside the hotel is a Wolfgang Puck restaurant. That's where I got to meet Wolfgang Puck. And when we did the podcast together [*The Flavor Flav Show*], we said we were going to do a chicken standoff one day. So I'm looking forward to doing it.

BLVR: Do you and Wolfgang Puck swap recipes?

FF: No. I don't think he's giving anybody any of his recipes. I do have a couple of recipes that I did put out there, but they're in my book. So you got to get my book, *Flavor Flav: The Icon, The Memoir*, and look at the back of that book, because I put out at least three real recipes.

BLVR: So you really like cooking?

FF: I sure do.

BLVR: What do you cook for yourself?

FF: My specialty is fried chicken. One day I want to have a franchise, a fried chicken franchise. But when I cook for myself, it's just normal things, you know? Like, I wake up in the morning and I take a whole pack of bacon and I cook a pack of bacon and I got to eat the whole pack, along with maybe some eggs and some bread?

BLVR: Do you do this under medical supervision? That sounds like a lot.

FF: Under my own medical supervision. It works for me, Melissa.

BLVR: Has there ever been a fried chicken you didn't like?

FF: I forgot where we were, but I ain't gonna lie, shit was absolutely nasty. I swear to goodness, the crust on it was so hard and damn near chipped my teeth. I know the way there, and I am never going back again.

BLVR: I read this question in *Bon Appétit*, but if you're having a dinner party and you've cooked all the food, which three people, dead or alive, would you like to invite over?

FF: To tell you the truth—I'm not trying to sound selfish but, yes, sometimes I do get very selfish—the main three people I would love to have there is me, myself, and I.

BLVR: You just want all your cooking to yourself?

FF: That's right. I want it all for myself.

IV. FLAVOR FLAV TWINKLE TOES FLINTSTONE

BLVR: OK, so if you don't want to share your food, who would be your dream guests for a Flavor Flav variety show or Las Vegas residency?

FF: I would want to get Megan Thee Stallion. I want to get Bruno Mars. I want to get Wiz Khalifa, Snoop, some of my old friends like Ice-T and Flo Rida. And some of my old influences that are still living, like Dionne Warwick and Patti LaBelle. I'm gonna get some movie actors like Robert De Niro coming through my show.

BLVR: So you would have all these people on your show, but you wouldn't have them for dinner?

FF: I would have them for dinner if they would eat my food. Nobody would leave my house with an empty stomach.

BLVR: You live in Las Vegas now, so do you go to any of the big shows? Did you ever see Siegfried and Roy?

FF: No, I've never seen Siegfried and Roy in person. I've seen them on television. But, you know, my good friend is Criss Angel and he has his show out there, *Mindfreak*. And Carrot Top is my boy. He's a funny character, man. I go down to his show sometimes. I also love the Jabbawockeez. Those guys got some dance moves!

BLVR: What about Celine Dion?

FF: No. And I still never got to the Boyz II Men show and I want to get down there. Gotta go see my Boyz II Men. I love those guys, man.

BLVR: They've been Boys II Men for so long, like, when are they going to become, like, Boys II Grandpas?

FF: Yeah. From Boys II Grandpas! Probably some of them are grandpas by now. That is a good one, man. Wait till I see them next time, man. I'll be like, *Yo, who got grandkids in your group?*

BLVR: You seem to be working a lot. What do you do for fun?

FF: I bowl a lot. I love going bowling. I'm a bowling junkie. Sometimes you can find me at the bowling alley two or three times a week. Four times a week sometimes.

BLVR: Do you own your own shoes?

FF: I sure do, and I own my own ball.

BLVR: What was your best score?

FF: The highest score that I ever had in my life was, like, I don't know, a 275 or 76 or something. But I only did it once.

BLVR: I don't really know bowling, but congratulations?

FF: They call me Flavor Flav Twinkle Toes Flintstone when I am at the bowling alley, OK? I'm a beast! I go full beast mode.

BLVR: Do you hype yourself up before you bowl?

FF: Sometimes. It depends on who I'm bowling against.

BLVR: When you, the quintessential hypeman, are hyping yourself up, what does that sound like?

FF: I ain't gonna lie, but I do a good job after I hype myself up, you know? Usually I don't lose.

BLVR: Does bowling count as exercise?

FF: Yes. It's exercise, but it's also a mental thing. Some people go to the bowling alley to knock pins down because they're stressed out. At the end of the bowling game, a lot of the stress is gone, 'cause they took it out on the pins instead of taking it out on people at home.

BLVR: It makes you wonder what was stressing Fred Flintstone out if he had to spend so much time in the bowling alley.

FF: That's right. He would've been going crazy with Barney [Rubble], that's for sure.

BLVR: You said you always wanted to be famous for music, and I know you just released a new song. Can you tell me about it?

FF: Yeah it's an EDM song called "Hands up in the Air." It's the first solo single that I've dropped in a very long time. I feel it's definitely, *definitely* a good record.

BLVR: What made you want to explore EDM?

FF: Well, I'm a musician, so I explore all kinds of music. I never put out an EDM record before so I said to myself: I can put out any kind of record I want and be successful. So that's why you got EDM.

BLVR: There has been a lot of crossover to country music. Maybe you should do a country song next!

FF: I did one a long time ago. Way back in 2000, 1999. The world never heard it, because my first album got cease-and-desisted, but the name of the song was "Harder than Ice."

BLVR: Do you remember how the song went?

FF: "I'm hotter than ice for you, baby. I hope our love will never end. Without you my world is like yellow snow, but with you it's white once again."

BLVR: Wow! I feel like you just need one reference to a truck or a love of tequila and fried chicken and you have the perfect country song.

FF: Yeah, *Git along, little doggie!*

BLVR: So if you're now in this age of exploring, since you're doing an EDM song, maybe you can resurrect that song and do a whole country crossover.

FF: Yep, that's right. I'm going to redo it anyway. I have a lot cooking. I'm getting ready to shock you. I'm going to shock you. I'm going to shock everybody. ✱

For years, the author was under the impression that her grandmother, the iconic poet Muriel Rukeyser, used Donnan Jeffers, son of another iconic poet, Robinson Jeffers, as a sperm bank, for the purposes of begetting a literary child. But was this the whole story?

IF ONE WOMAN TOLD THE TRUTH ABOUT HER LIFE

by **REBECCA RUKEYSER**

illustrations by **MADISON KETCHAM**

Sometime in 1969, my grandmother tried to decapitate her good friend Ella Winter. My father was there; I know that. I imagine him wearing the blue corduroy suit he wore at his wedding; I'm sure he didn't. I imagine him humiliated.

Muriel Rukeyser, so my father says, was not an accomplished drinker. But for some reason, that evening in San Francisco, shortly past the Summer of Love, she was drinking heavily.

She was at a party, among friends. But she started getting agitated, my father says, when the subject turned to Carmel-by-the-Sea. She lurched toward the hatchet in the basket of kindling when Ella Winter started mentioning the Jeffers family, who had lived in Carmel for fifty years at that point. And she grabbed the hatchet—now I'm imagining the running, and the lunge—and charged across the long-pile shag carpet, hatchet held over her head, aiming for the neck, when Ella Winter said something about Donnan Jeffers.

When my father relayed this, he didn't mention what Muriel did after she was pulled off Ella Winter,

or what she did after the hatchet was taken from her hands. She might have been contrite, or shaking with rage. He did say that Muriel had to be "forcibly restrained." He did mention that ("luckily, luckily") the blow was never struck.

What's for sure is that the reason his mother ran pell-mell toward Ella Winter in the middle of the boozy camaraderie, in the decline of the 1960s, was because she heard that Ella Winter was still being friendly with the man that had impregnated Muriel back in 1946: the man who had fathered my father.

People like to introduce Muriel Rukeyser, my paternal grandmother, in a couple of ways.

They like to use lists. Muriel was, as Adrienne Rich describes her in the introduction to *A Muriel Rukeyser Reader*, a "poet, first and foremost; but [also] a thinking activist, biographer, traveler, explorer of her country's psychic geography." Her poetry: labeled, among other things, as romantic, political, feminist, erotic, Whitmanesque. Muriel: poet, novelist, biographer, playwright, filmmaker, children's writer, bisexual, Jewish, single mother, and a tireless social activist.

"Anne Sexton," writes Laura Passin, "called her 'Muriel, mother of us all,' and Adrienne Rich named her 'our twentieth-century Coleridge, our Neruda, and more.'" Many people are introduced to Muriel through one of her most famous lines, well known even before it gained viral popularity during the #MeToo movement: "What would happen if one woman told the truth about her life? The world would split open."

It was not until he was in middle school that Muriel sat my father down and informed him that she'd been lying. My father's father was not the man that Muriel had described. My father's father was alive, not dead. He wasn't Jewish. He had never married Muriel; in fact, he was married to another woman. He was highly unlikely ever to resurface. His name was Donnan Jeffers.

My father remembers his reaction: "And my birthday? Is it still September twenty-fifth?"

Bill Rukeyser was born on September 25, 1947. He was conceived between Thanksgiving and New Year's Eve in the rowdy artistic epicenter of Carmel-by-the-Sea, where Donnan Jeffers was licking his wounds from the combination of his recent acrimonious divorce, being laid off from working in his ex-father-in-law's commercial pottery in Ohio, and the indignity of moving back in with Mommy and Daddy in his early thirties. But despite all this, Donnan was already holding sway over Carmel, drinking heavily, a malcontent bon viveur. He was already acting in the role he'd inhabit—and would make the cornerstone of his personality and his primary source of income—until his death: that of Robinson Jeffers's son.

"I consider Jeffers the most important American poet of the western third of the country—the great poet of the West," says former poet laureate of California Dana Gioia. He's not alone in that sentiment. When Robinson Jeffers is remembered fondly, it's as an ardent environmentalist, a poet who worked on a grand scale, composing epics about the California coast, where he and his family settled in 1919.

The Jeffers compound, known as Tor House, consists of a cluster of stone buildings on Carmel Point. It's an arresting place. The movement of the gray water is reflected by the movement of the gray marine layer surging inland. Between those layers of gray are black cypress trees and boulders, also gray.

This natural beauty, this feral, blasted landscape, is what's really credited with molding Jeffers's poetics, his defiant preference of nature to mankind, his preoccupation with hawks. *Rugged* is a word used with astounding frequency to describe him: his free verse is rugged; his features are "rugged and intense."

By 1932 he'd hit such a height of fame that his photo—rugged face against hewn stone—graced the cover of *Time*. It would be eighteen years before T. S. Eliot was on the cover of *Time*; this is how famous a poet Robinson Jeffers was in the early 1930s.

When my grandmother broke the news of my father's lineage to him, it was Robinson's name, not Donnan's, that she mentioned first.

"And my mother says something like, *Oh, by the way, I've got something to tell you.* And I can't remember the exact words but the net impact was *Everything that you think you know about your parenthood is not true. Here is the real truth. Have you ever heard of the poet Robinson Jeffers? You're his grandson.*"

I was at the end of my honeymoon when I decided to go to Tor House. We'd rented a house in the Mojave Desert, spending our days floating around the pool on inflatable mattresses, looking up at the pink-and-black mountains.

My husband was born in West Germany; he's Bavarian. I spent childhood summers in the Central Valley of California, indoors, in the air-conditioning, dreaming of living in Europe. Now that I live in Germany, things have changed. I own three prints of California landscapes. I now look at photos of the American West with such rapaciousness that I gnash my teeth. When I visit the United States, I tend to binge on it. I have become a German tourist.

"Why not," I asked my husband, "go from the desert up to the coast? We could see Big Sur, and Santa Cruz, and"—here I started looking at the Tor House Foundation website—"check out Carmel-by-the-Sea?" I found something called the Musical Tour of Tor House, celebrating the fact that "Tor House became a magnet for the musical, artistic and literary aristocracy of the 1920s through 1940s." I bought the two remaining tickets.

My husband said it sounded cheesy. I called my parents, who live near Carmel, in Davis. Was my mother interested in going? "That sounds horrible," she said. Was my father? I understood that he probably wasn't, I said, but I wanted to ask. After all, Muriel had been at Tor House in the 1940s.

"Sure," he said. "Why the hell not?"

Here is what Muriel told my father for the first thirteen years of his life: *Your father, before he died, was a Jewish schoolteacher named David Woolff. We married and then he got leukemia; it struck him fast and he was gone, just like that.*

I wondered if my father grew up hearing a lot of stories about David Woolff, the nice Jewish boy with a

37

name that essentially screams *nice Jewish boy*? "Actually, not too many," says my dad. "Grandma would tend to lapse into silence, and from a very early age one of the things I learned was when to shut up."

Muriel never publicly mentioned the name Donnan Jeffers. And it was only recently that my father did. Previously, he said simply that his mother "sought out the son of a famous poet."

Much later he met his half siblings, including the daughter from Donnan's failed first marriage. It was through his half sister that he first came into contact with a Jeffers scholar named James Karman, who, through inserting my father's name in a footnote in *The Collected Letters of Robinson Jeffers* (2015), first officially announced my father's paternity.

"I didn't name names," my father says, "until after Karman broke the news to a world that frankly doesn't care."

We drive down to Tor House the day before my father's seventy-fourth birthday. In September, moving from the heat of the interior of California to the chill of the marine layer is shocking. As we turn onto Highway 1, my dad asks me: Do I want to let the docents know who I am and maybe get the VIP tour? My father had been to Tor House once before, in 2017 or 2018, accompanied by Karman. He'd gotten to see the entire house; everyone had been very solicitous. Or: we could be surreptitious.

I choose to be surreptitious.

One of the things I've been highly aware of, being Muriel's granddaughter, is looking like Muriel's granddaughter. We have the same wide face. Broad,

perpetually tensed shoulders. A villainous arch to our eyebrows. And, as evidenced in some pictures, select old videos, a similarity in reaction: the movement of amusement across my face looks like it did on Muriel's—as does haughtiness, as does fury.

This wouldn't bother me quite so much, I think, if I weren't a writer. When I speak to Muriel fans, they tend to draw parallels. I know it's because they're so invested in Muriel, because they see Muriel everywhere they go and not just in me, but when a Muriel scholar recently said, "Your novel is called *The Seaplane on Final Approach*? But that's amazing—Muriel's first book was *Theory of Flight*, also about aviation!," my face registered, I'm sure, Muriel-like haughtiness.

My novel is not about aviation. My novel, I realize as I write this, is about destructive desire in a coastal corner of the American West.

Muriel and Robinson Jeffers first came into contact in 1944, when Muriel was staying at the home of her good friend Ella Winter, the woman she would later charge with a hatchet. The houses in Carmel-by-the-Sea are all called "cottages," a collection of achingly sweet little homes painted the colors of Jordan almonds and named like fairy-tale ships: Sea Lure, Salt Aire, Mission Belle. Ella Winter's cottage was called The Getaway.

Tor House isn't painted pink or mint or baby blue. It's gray, craggy granite, as is the adjacent structure, Hawk Tower. The legend goes that as Robinson Jeffers constructed Hawk Tower, a hawk kept daily watch over his progress. When he was finished, after he had applied the

mortar and laid the last stone by hand, the hawk took flight.

In 1933, Jeffers published a book of poetry called *Give Your Heart to the Hawks and Other Poems*. One of his famous poems is called "Rock and Hawk." Another of his famous poems, "Hurt Hawks," contains the line "I'd sooner, except the penalties, kill a man than a hawk." (The poem is about him killing a hawk.)

Robinson Jeffers would rather kill a man than a hawk. This fact has something to do with the decline in his popularity in the years leading up to and during World War II. When Muriel met him, he was at a bit of a low point.

This was because Robinson Jeffers's philosophy, which he dubbed "inhumanism," urged people to look away from the squalor of human life and toward nature. When faced with the madness of the human world, with its murder and greed and corruption, the only even remotely sensible thing to do, for Jeffers, was to be indifferent to human struggle. He preferred the specter of a god who was aloof and radiant, who hadn't wrought man in His image, and might resemble something other than human.

Robinson Jeffers, as a by-product of his inhumanism, was an America Firster. He didn't want the United States to enter World War II. This fact torpedoed his popularity, and he was accused of having Fascist sympathies. The mournful newsreel voice in a Robinson Jeffers documentary intones, "Except for a small and intensely loyal Robinson Jeffers cult of close friends and admirers, his followers dwindled until he suffered almost complete obscurity." This is when Muriel met him.

In 1936, a year after Jeffers published the volume of poetry in which "Rock and Hawk" appears, Muriel, aged twenty-two, did a few things that permanently altered the shape of her life and writing.

She drove to West Virginia to witness the aftermath of one of the worst industrial tragedies in American history, the Hawks Nest Tunnel disaster at Gauley Bridge, where an estimated thousand people died of silicosis as a result of gross negligence on the part of the Union Carbide Company. She wrote a poem sequence about it—potentially her most famous, lauded work—called "The Book of the Dead." Later that year, she traveled to Barcelona, witnessed the outbreak of the Spanish Civil War, and was evacuated on a fishing boat that sailed, under cover of night, to France.

This is when Muriel became a *poet of witness*, a term that would come to define her. "Rukeyser," writes Natasha Trethewey in her introduction to 2021's *The Essential Muriel Rukeyser*, "over the course of her long career—a life of conscientious reckoning with the self and the world—would bear witness to many of the most pressing issues of the century with the clarity and moral authority of one whose life was boldly and fully lived."

Muriel spent part of World War II working on home-front propaganda for the Office of War Information. Then, in 1944, she met—sought out—Robinson Jeffers, hawk fan and staunch isolationist.

My father understands his conception as "like a trip to the Gap. Muriel was shopping for genes."

His understanding of the situation is that Muriel wanted to beget a poet, or at least conceive a child with a man who had poetry somewhere, somehow, in his bloodline.

But why this particular poet? Why was Muriel, poet of witness and politics, activist, Communist, anti-Fascist, palling around with the family of Robinson Jeffers, America Firster, inhumanist, full of Fascist leanings? It's not like Robinson was still affecting the tidal pull of absolute fame and influence. His followers, remember, had dwindled.

Ella Winter loaned her The Getaway in 1944; Muriel met Robinson. Muriel returned to The Getaway in 1945. Muriel returned, again, to The Getaway that fateful winter of 1946, going to whatever party was suggested, strains of the new Christmas novelty song "Let It Snow" rising through the floorboards, Pacific storms lashing at the windows.

In my father's understanding of events, Muriel was filled with an unshakable confidence that her baby would have the perfect mix: a little poetry from Muriel; a little poetry, albeit once removed, from Robinson.

Muriel's thinking at the time, according to my dad: "If we're talking genes, creativity is inherited. Fascism is not."

He continues, "I mean, this is one of those things where there's so little data that I think you, Rebecca, can speculate as much as you want. And nobody can possibly definitively contradict you."

There are no photos allowed within the fenced perimeter of Tor House, certainly none within the confines of the house. You can photograph some of the two thousand cypresses, eucalyptuses, and Monterey pines planted by the Jefferses from the vantage point outside the gate.

Our docent tells us that the Jefferses, Una and Robinson, met in a class on Goethe's *Faust* at the University of Southern California. Robinson's German was impeccable. Una was already married when she met Robinson, explains our docent. He was monosyllabic, misanthropic, lean, and—so says the docent, so says everybody—"ruggedly good-looking." They started an affair. It lasted six, seven turbulent years. Then, even once Una and Robinson were finally married, they were plagued by scandal, so they decided to start fresh in coastal Carmel. The docent, I can tell, loves the story.

She takes a moment to ask us where we're from. I live in Germany. My father lives in Davis. We're surreptitious. When asked what we do, my father says, "Retired." I say, "I'm a teacher." These are truthful statements, and also not, but nobody can possibly definitively contradict us.

In photos Donnan Jeffers is a louche; every time I think back I remember him wearing a cravat, but no: there's a shirt, a tie, and a creamy scarf. He has slack, opiated lips and pale, hooded eyes.

Donnan was slight; his twin brother, Garth, was broad. He was lazy and indulgent; Garth went on cattle drives and became a forester. At one point in all this, Robinson said to Muriel, or so my father was told, "You chose the wrong twin."

He tried a number of careers; he failed at most of them. What he ended up being, what his personal and professional identity became, was Robinson Jeffers's son. He and his wife, Lee, lived in Tor House for the rest of his life, maintaining the property and helping establish the Robinson Jeffers Tor House Foundation, a non-profit that preserves Tor House and runs tours, including the Musical Tour of Tor House.

Donnan's drinking increased steadily throughout his life. He ended up dying at sixty-five, falling down the stairs at Tor House in a drunken stupor. The staircase at Tor House isn't even very steep.

"Is that just a story?" I ask.

"I think you can take that to the bank," says my dad.

When poet and editor Kate Daniels was attempting to write a biography of Muriel (the project was ultimately abandoned), she interviewed Donnan's widow, Lee. She asked Lee about Muriel, and about the possibility that Donnan had sired Muriel's son.

No, said Lee. Donnan could not possibly have slept with Muriel *because Donnan would never fuck a Jewess.*

My father backtracks. He wants the wording to be exactly right. Lee Jeffers might not have been so virulent or crude. The gist of it, though, was that Donnan was anti-Semitic. *We all know how Donnan felt about Jews* might have been what she said; impossible to father a child with one.

We all know how not just Donnan but all the Jefferses felt about Jews. We know because it's right there in the three volumes of *The Collected Letters of Robinson Jeffers, with Selected Letters of Una Jeffers.*

In 1944, the year that poet of witness Muriel Rukeyser first met the isolationist Robinson Jeffers, she wrote a poem called "To Be a Jew in the Twentieth Century," which begins:

> To be a Jew in the twentieth
>   century
> Is to be offered a gift. If you refuse,
> Wishing to be invisible, you
>   choose
> Death of the spirit, the stone
>   insanity.

It's a popular poem in many Reform Jewish prayer books. It was in the siddur at my synagogue when I was growing up.

On my dad's birth certificate his father is listed as David Jefferson Woolff. This is the only clue Muriel left as to the identity of her son's father: a tradition in the sorority of unmarried mothers claiming widowhood was to conceal the father's real name in a fake one. It's a simple exercise in erasure: *David Jefferson Woolff* cleverly concealing *D. Jeffers.*

David Woolff, need we explain, is the consummate Jewish American mate. Does he have some literary pedigree? No matter. He was a schoolteacher; he loved children and learning—that's what my father needed to know. David Woolff, newly married, rejoicing at the triumph over Nazism and probably planning on building a cabin upstate for his bride and baby, would have fucked a Jewess.

The docent at Tor House explains Robinson's philosophy of inhumanism: "We are all one. And maybe we're of less importance than the rocks and the ocean and the plants, because we are a destructive presence on the earth."

The poem she chooses to illustrate inhumanism is an early one, "Continent's End." It's the one poem she reads aloud; the other poems she wants us, the guests at Tor House, to read aloud ourselves.

> Mother, though my song's measure
> is like your surf-beat's ancient
> rhythm I never learned it of you.
>
> Before there was any water there
> were tides of fire, both our tones
> flow from the older fountain.

"Mother," the docent explains, refers to the Pacific Ocean.

If Muriel was interested in using Donnan as a sperm bank, if she was indeed "shopping for genes," it might have had something to do with her understanding of her own ancestry. Muriel was the daughter of a former bookkeeper and a crooked cement magnate. She mentions her humble lineage often, and dismissively, throughout her work.

She also mentions a literary ancestor, one her bookkeeper mother told her she was related to: Rabbi Akiba, who is famous for including the erotic Song of Songs in the canon and for reciting the Shema Yisrael as he was being flayed by Roman soldiers.

With this, Muriel is bound by a hereditary link not only to poetry, but to poetry that exalts the holiness of carnality and the body. Her ancestor is a rabbi who martyred himself not only in an act of resistance, but in an act of resistance accompanied by indelible literary recitation.

Before the musical part of the Musical Tour of Tor House begins, before our docent starts playing on "Una's beautifully restored 1905 Steinway" and her husband starts singing in his wavering Irish baritone, we're led out of the back gate. Robinson, our docent explains, "had a personal relationship with the rocks and talked to them and wrote poems to them." She wants to show us a boulder.

It's also the rock that the Jefferses used to picnic beside before Tor House was constructed, before they'd bought the property, when Robinson and Una were living in a log cabin in central Carmel-by-the-Sea and the twin boys were still infants. It became the cornerstone of Tor House.

Robinson, naturally, wrote a poem to this rock. The docent, who has been picking people to read poems—the poem to Robinson's dead bulldog, the poem that tells people to leave poets alone and not invite them to parties—chooses my father to read "To the Rock That Will Be a Cornerstone of the House."

In the poem, Robinson contemplates what the rock experienced before he arrived. He brings the rock some milk and honey, some wine, and pours the offering into the moss growing from its cracked surface. He thinks of the rock's long history and offers himself and his future: the rock is going to have the task of supporting his house, helping shelter his family.

This is the poem my dad reads, and I'm worried he might choke up. "How dear you will be to me when I too grow old, old comrade." But my dad's reading voice is steady and sounds, if anything, slightly mocking.

The poem "Trinity Churchyard," subtitled "for my mother and her ancestor Akiba," is included in Muriel's last poetry collection, *The Gates*. It was published in 1976. Muriel was sixty-two years old, still thinking about the Akiba myth. It's clear that the idea of lineage, a heritage of notable acts, was important to her. There's a sense of reverence there, and a sense of crafted destiny.

I can see, following from the idea of her ancestor, the idea that her child's father's background would mold his future. That you can do more than influence your baby's probable height or eye color or likelihood of high blood pressure when you choose your mate.

But this is also the part that upsets me: the idea of Muriel trying to beget a poet. The year of her tryst with Donnan was 1946. The atrocities in Europe had been laid bare: everyone knew about Jews being eradicated not only because we were undesirable but also because of the threat that we'd breed with non-Jews. People knew about the Nazi *Lebensborn* program: young, blond German women selected to conceive with SS officers, then sent to rest homes during their pregnancy to ensure they'd safely deliver strong, lusty Aryan babies. People knew about the experiments. They knew about the fetishization of a pure bloodline. They knew about the idea of building through genetic specificity, creating a child that would have the ideal traits of athleticism and industry and blondness.

Everyone knew this. So why, in 1946, did my grandmother decide—if you believe my father's understanding that she was shopping for genes—to cook up a literary baby? Why—in this hedonistic season where I imagine, outside

twinkling houses, conversations held in the dark, clutching the lapels of a coat before the black silhouette of a cypress stamping the black of the overcast sky— did she sleep with Donnan Jeffers to make this genetically fit poet?

That's not what Muriel said she did, however. She says she simply fell in love and got pregnant.

This was a surprise to me; I had never heard this. I'd only ever heard my father's account of the story, and I'd assumed for my entire life that his glibness—*shopping for genes*—was Muriel's. I'd grown up with an image of Muriel walking around, smugly patting her pregnant belly: *Look what I got here*. But that, I guess, is probably not what she did.

I ask: "Did she say anything to you—I mean, your line about shopping for genes?"

My father answers: "That's entirely my line. Basically, her line was that [Donnan] was the love of her life and it had gone wrong. And it had been a terrible and tragic disappointment when she learned that he was marrying somebody else. That was her line for the rest of her life."

I had spent thirty-six years telling everyone that Muriel used Donnan like a sperm bank. I had never questioned my dad's narrative, never assumed that love or heartbreak was part of the equation.

The windows are kept open during the musical part of the Musical Tour of Tor House. It gets progressively colder and I try unsuccessfully to fold my skirt double and pull my jacket down over my legs. We're given a little revue of music from the heyday of Robinson Jeffers's popularity: "Let the Rest of the World Go By," Duke Ellington's "Moonglow," the Gershwins' "Our Love Is Here to Stay." Between songs, the docent reads us Robinson Jeffers poems. The living room at Tor House is low-ceilinged. It's filled with books and one wall is decorated with a large drawing of the twins, Donnan and Garth, as children. I'm feeling cynical—toward the fetishization of these Tor House parties, toward the reverence directed toward my America Firster granddad and his anti-Semitic family—but two things keep pricking through the membrane of my contempt with real and vivid emotion.

One is the view from the paned window. It's the slope of the cliff down to the water, which is frothing against a jagged collection of low-tide rocks. From the right, the fingers of a cypress intrude. There are too many clouds to see the horizon line, so it lacks that particular tang of immensity, but there's the swarming motion of the marine layer moving inland. It's beautiful, and I'm homesick for it already.

Two, and this upsets me, is Robinson's poetry. I've never read it before. Now that I'm hearing it, seated under a pencil sketch of five-year-old Donnan, I'm mortified to find that I deeply love Robinson Jeffers's early poems.

Muriel made mention of Donnan in her poetry, although never by name. One example is from the first stanza of "Desdichada," a title that translates as something like "unfortunate wretch," from *Breaking Open* (1973):

For that you never acknowledged
    me, I acknowledge
the spring's yellow detail, the every
    drop of rain,
the anonymous unacknowledged
    men and women.
The shine as it glitters in our
    child's wild eyes,
one o'clock at night.

If we assume the poem's speaker is Muriel—the speaker in her poems is often Muriel—she's talking to Donnan about my father's wild eyes. These aren't the words of someone easily happy to have been impregnated by the handsome, soused local sperm donor. This is Muriel as a woman scorned, a woman who was abandoned while pregnant. She's heartbroken.

Despite the chill in the room, and the citric smell of kelp the wind brings in, the docent urges us to imagine the living room filled with the kind of artistic guests Tor House attracted. She lists names—Edna St. Vincent Millay, Sinclair Lewis, George Sterling, Dylan Thomas, Martha Graham. Imagine them in the throes of a raucous party, the kind that misanthropic Robinson would have hated.

The gas lamps are all lit. Una is playing the piano. The fire is roaring, voices are roaring above the fire. It's too loud inside to hear the wind, or the water, or the crows, or the needles of the cypresses against the window. People cluster by the fireplace, drinking Irish whiskey. Bodies are spilling up the stairs, some into the corner with the desk referred to as "Una's Alcove." Someone leans against Una's melodeon, which gives a horsey wheeze, which is echoed by

laughter. A cigarette butt is thrown into the fireplace, releasing a spray of sparks; a cigarette is lit from the flame of a candle. Whiskey is dribbled down a double-breasted jacket and artfully flicked off with manicured nails. Red lipstick is reapplied by someone using the reflection on the black window, faces swim in and out of the rippled antique panes. A pair of heeled Oxfords slides on the staircase leading upstairs, an ass in a tweed skirt sits down hard, there's a hush, she's OK, and everyone cheers with wine-stained teeth. Una is sent for more whiskey, and someone ambushes her, kissing her underneath the mistletoe, and it's played for laughs because Una's old enough to be somebody's grandmother.

My father recently confessed that he had long harbored a secret wish. Wouldn't it have been nice, he thought, if he had actually been Robinson's son? A son of the poet, instead of a son of a man who spent his life as The Son of the Poet? After all, Robinson had cheated on Una before.

But no—my father took a cheekswab DNA test and the results came back: you have a half sister in England and her father is Donnan Jeffers.

When we leave Tor House, I ask my dad what he thought of the tour. He inhales. Then, with a sideways glance and a slight angling of his head, adopting a tone of serene, thoughtful diplomacy—something he does, that I've caught my nephew doing, and that I've seen Muriel do in videos, when they want to express withering scorn—he says, "I enjoyed looking out the living room window and watching the pelicans playing."

The first stanza of Muriel's "Desdichada" goes on:

Disinherited, annulled, finally
    disacknowledged
and all of my own asking.
    I keep that wild dimension
of life and making and the spasm
upon my mouth as I say this word
    of acknowledge
to you forever.   *Ewig.*   Two
o'clock at night.

The disacknowledgment Muriel is referencing here: Donnan not acknowledging the existence of my father.

But then I read it again, with the sensation I often have while reading Muriel Rukeyser, something like the movement of a puck across an air hockey table: the movement of one meaning frictionlessly becoming another meaning entirely.

Disinherited, annulled, finally
    disacknowledged
and all of my own asking.

This line complicates the heartbreak, and Muriel's statement that losing Donnan was losing the love of her life. *All of my own asking.*

I stick on this; I circle back around it. Did Muriel ask Donnan to refuse to acknowledge my father? Or the fact that they'd had a wild night together, or a full-fledged affair? Did Muriel, who grieved Donnan to the extent that she refused to speak with my father about him, shut herself within her grief and shut her child out of knowledge about his father?

The more people I talk to about Muriel's tryst with Donnan, the more theories I hear. It could have been that Donnan provoked in Muriel the thunderclap of sudden, defenseless love. Or that she had tried to seduce Robinson and failed; that drunk Donnan was an easy conquest. Or that she told Donnan outright, *I want a baby, and I want you to give it to me*, and he agreed. Or that, having checked the attributes she wanted in a mate and propelled by a deluded and icky understanding of poetry as a genetic trait, she used him like a sperm bank.

But maybe, also, if she was looking for poetic genes, she didn't acknowledge this to herself. She didn't allow herself to think of her affair with Donnan Jeffers as anything less than an affair—of the heart, of the heart manifested in the body.

So far, two biographies of Muriel Rukeyser have been abandoned by their authors. My father's theory is that

the biographers started their projects totally smitten with Muriel but grew disenchanted. "The more they got to the original source material and interviews, the more they saw the flaws, the contradictions, the unpleasant sides of her personality. And at a certain point, you know, the facts and the myth just didn't jibe, and if they were in love with her, they couldn't continue." But, he admits, "that's a theory based on not a whole hell of a lot."

There is something there, though: that frictionless slide, that negation, again and again. A Jew in the twentieth century, in 1946, kissing an avowed anti-Semite at a Christmas party. A young poet repulsed by political inaction, besotted by a gone-to-seed poet whose legacy is isolationism. A woman whose generosity and kindness were balanced by fits of rage, a tendency to feel perpetually betrayed. She wasn't completely strong, was often self-pitying; she relished and then rejected herself, again and again.

Maybe Muriel was terrified by the prospect of the truth splitting the world open. She rewrote her own history frequently. She waited decades after her son's birth to write cryptic lines about Donnan.

And, lest we forget, she grabbed a hatchet from the pile of kindling and ran drunkenly, full throttle, filled with pain and anger, full of an amount of theatricality we'll never be able to extricate from an amount of real passion, toward Ella Winter, with one plan: to chop off Ella Winter's head because she'd kept in contact with Donnan Jeffers. ✴

TOO MUCH AND THEREFORE NOTHING

A NEW POEM

by Jenny Xie

The plot's restless.

Newness grown
stiff from disuse.
To believe to have lived
through the end

of something
and still to remain
in that tight ruse
of the habitual.

Slice a day open:
the padded announcing,
coils of debts and balances
and that dull spray

of the first person singular.

My god, the thick paste
of the past
collapsing fresh
from the tube!

You envy children's eyes,
how they chew
on parts of the world
that lack firmness.

And what was it
the lama said last week
over Zoom?

The more he practices,
year after year
after year,
the more ordinary
he grows.

You understood
this was welcome.

Meager ambitions
require discipline—
pouring the slosh
of desire
over and over
until it thins.

It's like this:
time is this
and that.

And the ordinary
is hardest
to dream, yes.

Much easier to pull
at the tufts
of a thousand illusions
falling through one hour
into the next.

MICHAEL IMPERIOLI

[ACTOR, WRITER, MUSICIAN]

"I REALLY WANTED THE MAGIC."

Tibetan Buddhist concepts Michael Imperioli discusses in this interview:
Gom: *to familiarize or habituate*
Nirvana: *looking within the nature of your own mind*
Samsara: *a looking out, projecting, being lost in projections*
Karunā: *a tender heart*
Tendrel: *an auspicious coincidence or circumstance*

About an hour after we sat down at a sidewalk table at Caffe Dante in *Greenwich Village, each drinking a pot of green tea, a self-proclaimed huge fan interrupted our conversation, saying he hated to do so, but "I loved your work in* The Sopranos." *This happens to Michael Imperioli. People know Christopher Moltisanti. They know Spider from* Goodfellas. *Both characters—Tony Soprano's nervy, wide-eyed nephew and the Scorsese gangster—have some things in common: they're earnest greenhorns caught up in chaotic violence, and at this point, they're very much in Imperioli's past. His presence now is calm and patient, an absolute flip side to the energy of those two, but their roles still follow him, even as he's gone on to shows like* Californication *and* The White Lotus. *When the fan approached us, Imperioli shook his hand, receiving him gracefully, and later admitted to having no control over what people do with his image. "It is what it is," he says.*

Illustration by Kristian Hammerstad

This chill is no trickery. To use a metaphor Imperioli is fond of: if you're digging for water in the desert, you can dig either a thousand holes one foot deep, or one hole a thousand feet deep. It seemed to me that he knew how to do both, how to bring an immediate presence into everything he did, every role he's acted, and every small encounter. Imperioli's a man who spends a lot of time sitting patiently with his own mind. I wanted to better understand his framework.

Where the thousand holes are concerned, Imperioli's a multi-hyphenate: He came up in New York City's downtown arts scene in the '80s, playing in noise and punk groups, and acting in theaters and small-budget films. Since The Sopranos *ended, his own projects have had more purchase: his 2009 film,* Hungry Ghosts; *his 2018 novel,* The Perfume Burned His Eyes; *and his ongoing three-piece rock band, Zopa—all of them dowse for the same water. A real capaciousness carries through all his work, a feeling of immediacy and constant curiosity.*

When I first heard it, I thought the hole metaphor was about picking a lane, but the truth is, as long as you dig, there's water. A key part of Imperioli's divination comes from Tibetan Buddhism. He took vows and he practices. He teaches a weekly meditation class. The name of his rock trio translates from the Tibetan as "patience." Buddhism has become part of everything he does. He's glad to be a perpetual student.

Imperioli's unabashed love for heroes and teachers, of which his social media offers daily evidence, had me watching John Cassavetes's films after we talked. Whenever Cassavetes appeared on-screen, I thought, Damn, they're the same guy. What I recognized was this magic of immediacy that performers can have when they're completely tapped into the moment, when it feels like there's no separation between thought and expression. How to live safely in that moment for a lifetime is the real work of so many artists. Imperioli would never say there's just one way to do it, but that Tibetan Buddhism has given him a particular tool kit. It's where he landed after a long spiritual search, and it's what has sustained him in the artistic depths. His openness is one of the most powerful and particular things about him. It's a feeling strong enough to make fans stop him on the street because they feel an urgent need to share something—even if it's just a moment.

Our conversation started when Imperioli saw a copy of The Diamond Cutter Sutra *inside my bag.*

—Hayden Bennett

I. A VIBE

MICHAEL IMPERIOLI: That was the first Buddhist book I ever bought, *The Diamond Sutra*, when I was nineteen.

THE BELIEVER: What got you into it?

MI: Jack Kerouac.

BLVR: *Dharma Bums*?

MI: Just in general, but I couldn't penetrate it. I still have the copy.

BLVR: Yeah, it's difficult. Especially how it's formatted with all these commentaries. Reading it the past few days, I was like, Just give me the sutra. Tell me what the sutra is.

MI: That might not make it easier.

BLVR: No, it doesn't work. You have to get into the whole nested thing. Teachers quoting teachers.

MI: With the books, yeah. A lot of it's following actual teachers' instructions: what they emphasize, making a connection with them. Devotion is a big part of Tibetan Buddhism. Not in an obsequious or sycophantic way—it's much more about trusting that this path is right for you. This person, the teacher you've made, is going to bring you along that path. In the Tibetan Buddhist tradition, your own teacher is more important than the Buddha.

BLVR: The teacher is the lineage.

MI: Yes, 100 percent. For me, that's what separated Buddhism from a lot of other paths. The lineage is almost a safety mechanism, because you know it's not somebody just making it up as they go along: a little of this, a little of that. It's more like this is how it's been done. Generation to generation, teacher to student, teacher to student—for so many years.

BLVR: Even the phrase *taking refuge*. There's a lot of trust in it.

MI: Yeah, it's a good phrase, right? In the meditation class we do, someone asked a question on Sunday about someone who was a Catholic: raised Catholic, is a Catholic. They asked, "Are they compatible? Can you be both?" I was told you can't be both. You don't have to be a Buddhist to study Buddhism and to enjoy the teachings or apply the teachings or to meditate. But Buddhism is not a self-proclaimed thing. Being a Buddhist means you have taken refuge in the Buddha, the Dharma, or the teachings, and the Sangha, the congregation. You commit to what those vows mean.

BLVR: The tradition seems to make it feel pretty safe.

MI: Oh, I think so. It's really important, because we're so fallible as human beings that without the discipline of the lineage and the tradition and the requirements and the respect and the commitment and obligation you have for it—without that, things can… You've seen *Wild Wild Country*?

BLVR: I haven't.

MI: Osho, Rajneesh, was a guy who had lot of spiritual knowledge. But there wasn't a lineage. He had no guru. It became this cult of personality and went completely bonkers.

BLVR: Lou Reed, in *The Perfume Burned His Eyes*, felt a little like a dangerous teacher—it's not his intent, but the main character, who's just seventeen, is charmed by his way of being, how close Reed lives to his art.

MI: Too much voltage at that age. You know, that's really what it was. I don't think it was necessarily toxic or poisonous. It was just too much too soon. I call it voltage… energy, right? That intensity.

BLVR: At seventeen it's really tempting to jump over everything.

MI: That's exactly how I felt. You want to jump over this stuff. I didn't go to college, because after high school I was gonna go to SUNY-Albany, and I went up for the orientation weekend in the summer. I was like, This is just kind of like an extension of high school. They are just living in fucking dorms and not at home. I was like, I don't, I really don't feel like doing this.

Instead, I wound up going to acting school here, which was great. There were mostly people in their twenties, thirties, forties. That made all the difference for me. I wanted to be around people who were not kids anymore, who were adults and doing adult things.

BLVR: Was your family resistant?

MI: No, they were fine. They kind of understood. They also knew I was too stubborn. There was only so much control they had anyway. But they were very supportive and still are—and they're still here, which is nice.

BLVR: Is acting school where you met John Ventimiglia?

MI: Yeah, I met John. I met a guy named Tom Gilroy, who's an independent filmmaker—he was a really big influence on me. He was twenty-three and had just come from Boston College, where he was a DJ and he played in bands. We started a band together, started producing theater together, and started writing. He was a lot older and knew more about music, punk, literature, and film and stuff. I wasn't exposed to anything out of the mainstream until I was seventeen.

BLVR: The whole group in *Cabaret Maxime* does feel like it came up together.

MI: Yeah, I met Nick Sandow a few years after that. The director, Bruno de Almeida—we met in 1996. We did three movies: *On the Run* here in New York, and then *The Lovebirds* and *Cabaret Maxime* in Lisbon. Nick directed a lot of the plays when we had the theater. My wife and I opened Studio Dante [*points at the* CAFFE DANTE *sign above*] after Caffe Dante.

BLVR: *Cabaret Maxime* got me thinking about directors who come from theater with a crew. Fassbinder, Cassavetes…

MI: Yeah, Cassavetes was teaching an acting class, an improv class. Do you know that story? He was on a late-night radio show in New York. A guy named Jean Shepherd used to do this middle-of-the-night radio show with artists and celebrities. And Cassavetes started talking about an improv they were working on in his class. He said, "You know, if you want to see a good movie, people should send us money. We'll make a movie about this." People started sending dollar bills and then he felt obligated to start shooting *Shadows*.

BLVR: Is he still your favorite?

MI: Yeah, he'll always be my favorite just because he has a lot of compassion for his characters. The lines of what's bad and what's good get muddied. He understands that people are searching. I mean, in *The Killing of a Chinese Bookie* there are gangsters, but even there, Timothy Carey's character, when it's time to kill Ben Gazzara, he can't do it. He chickens out and becomes something else. I think he really had a lot of compassion for people in general.

The aesthetic is just gorgeous for someone who doesn't like to say that he has an aesthetic. It's beautiful. As a writer, he's incredibly underrated. A lot of the people I've met that worked with him say he wrote most of that stuff. It wasn't just, like, turn the camera on and actors going off.

BLVR: People assume most of it was improv?

MI: Yeah, all the time. It has that feeling.

BLVR: It does.

MI: And he was an actor. So the critics figure actors aren't that bright, so he probably didn't write it. Or that he wasn't really a filmmaker, because he didn't make Hollywood movies. He made these things that some people consider very indulgent. I think of them more as experiences. They were a completely new experience for me. I had seen *Gloria*—but that was a studio picture—when I was young. Anthology Film Archives, sometime in the '80s—I think late '80s?—did a retrospective. That was the first time I saw *A Woman Under the Influence*; *The Killing of a Chinese Bookie*. I had never seen anything like that, to the point where it was like a dream. You weren't really sure how much time had passed: Is this the beginning of the movie? Is this the middle? Is this the end? I still watch those movies. And they still challenge me. I mean, I've seen some of them twenty times.

BLVR: I went to the Rubin the other day, and the shrine on the third floor made me think of *The Killing*

of a Chinese Bookie because of all the red, the stage curtains. There's a certain intensity, really: it's a vibe.

MI: It's a vibe. I mean, that's how the shrine or the temple is designed. The thangka paintings are designed with a certain sacred geometry that corresponds to, like, the rods and cones in your eyes. Immediately, when you look at a thangka painting, the geometry of it connects to your sense faculties in a way to bring you into meditation: basically, to be in contact with your own mind in a deeper way.

BLVR: There's a lot of magic to *The Killing of a Chinese Bookie*—stage magic. Have you gotten much into or read much about Buddhist magic?

MI: Yeah. I mean, listen. Vajrayana Buddhism, or Tantric Buddhism, is primarily what Tibetan Buddhism is. It's really Buddhist mysticism. I mean, without a doubt. You can't really define it in any other way.

BLVR: Filmmakers can channel some magic. Assayas is somebody who often gets into this, what it means to live a little bit in the spirit world.

MI: I think in its purest form, art definitely has a connection to those things. I mean, part of *The Perfume Burned His Eyes* was really about how the character of Lou is almost like a shaman. Not intentionally, but he's living so far out of society, in a way, through his drug use and his psychological state and his choices.

Yet he is in the world and he's creating. So he's in touch with something that's really extraordinary and creating something tangible: a song or an album that people can actually listen to. I think when you're really in touch with certain truths, there is some magic to that. If you get out of the way, magical things happen.

II. GOM

BLVR: You've talked about taking Carlos Castaneda literally, the magic he writes about. I'm interested in what that can do, that belief.

MI: That was before I got into Buddhism. I really wanted the magic. I really did. And I believed that was possible. It's funny: sometimes when I'm in LA, in

Westwood, I drive by his house, which is on Pandora Avenue, where he practiced with the three witches and stuff like that. It's not far off Santa Monica Boulevard, but it's surrounded by hedges. I don't know who owns it now.

I just found it so fascinating that this lineage that had existed for centuries and centuries was still alive and that this guy stumbled into it. Which I do think he did. I'm not sure how much of what happened in those books is literally true. But I'm sure a lot of it is. There's a screenwriter, a novelist named Bruce Wagner…

BLVR: Oh, sure.

MI: You know him? He was a student of Castaneda. He wrote a book that's one of the best books I've ever read, called—

BLVR: The novel about LA?

MI: No, *The Empty Chair.* The one about LA he put me in.

BLVR: Like, full name?

MI: Yeah. I'm not really sure how I was portrayed, if he was being cynical or if he was being kind. I still don't know.

BLVR: Did you look at it?

MI: I did. I just can't tell. I didn't read the whole book.

BLVR: How do you relate to your image being out there? Christopher's a good example. I mean, is it just distance, something from the past?

MI: You know, when I got on social media, and during the pandemic, when I saw how much of a presence that character was in people's consciousness, especially among young people—I really wasn't aware of that. I kind of said, Well, why don't you just own that a little bit and use it to get your other stuff out there?

BLVR: That seems graceful.

MI: Yeah, it is what it is. Some people just see me as that. There's nothing you can do to ever change it. And I get that

too. I can't have it on my terms. I can't have your perception on my terms. Once you give it out, it's done, right?

BLVR: I've certainly struggled with the fact that once you write and publish something, it's out of your control.

MI: Completely, completely out of your control. Once it's out, you know, it is what it is. You post something about meditation and people comment with *Sopranos* quotes and stuff like that. You can't be like, They don't get it. It's just part of the whole thing.

BLVR: How often is the meditative mindset with you? I'm thinking about a student who asked the Dalai Lama, "What's the best time to meditate and how long should you do it?" And the response was "All the time."

MI: Yeah, well the point of meditation is not just for while you're on the cushion. It's for life and for living. You're practicing so you can bring a certain level of mindful awareness to your life and your motives. My understanding of what total enlightenment and full enlightenment are is that that becomes your state. Period.

You're in that level of awareness—and not just that level of awareness, but also I guess the realization of the truth of existence, interdependence, impermanence, and nonduality. The view of Buddhism is just completely realized in every waking moment.

The Tibetan word for meditation is *gom*, which means "to familiarize, to habituate." So what are you habituating? You're habituating your connection to your mind. Someone once said nirvana is looking within at the nature of your own mind. Samsara is looking out, projecting, being lost in projections. That's basically the only difference.

BLVR: You've talked about how playing a certain guitar over time with a certain kind of music—

MI: Will change the molecular structure of the guitar, yeah.

BLVR: That feels related to sitting to practice. Practicing for a long time. Practice becoming the default mode.

MI: Karmically as well. Karma is related to the actions of body, speech, and mind, right? You create karma through the actions of body, speech, and mind. And you experience a result of karma not just from actions of this lifetime, but from prior lifetimes as well.

Mental habit is very hard to get out of. The way you see things, the way you react to certain people. Addiction.

BLVR: It's a very deep groove.

MI: Addiction is a deep groove. That's a good way to put it.

BLVR: Do you feel like there's karma to representation in art? When you write something and show the shadow side and show violence.

MI: Is it negative karma?

BLVR: Is there a difference? Between negative karma and putting out negative things in the world?

MI: I think it depends on your intention. You know, if you make a film with a certain degree of violence, you can be a sadist and say, *I want people to suffer. I want people to really be revolted when they see this.* Well, maybe that's a negative intention, and if so it will create negative karma.

A good example for me is *Goodfellas*, right? Not because I'm in it or anything, but I think it is a really brilliant movie. I don't think Scorsese's intentions were negative at all. His intentions were to express a certain way of life that he had some familiarity with as a kid and was connected to through his ethnicity and heritage.

The opening of the movie is a flash-forward, right, to later on? It's the brutal murder of Billy Batts. After that, the story starts again, but from the chronological beginning, it's very kind of, [*snaps his fingers*] "Mack the Knife" or whatever. Rags to riches. Tony Bennett. Everyone's young, it's kind of innocent and still fun. It's before the coke and the psychosis and the sadism. He put that flash-forward up front to say, *Before you start having fun, remember: this is what this is about.* I think his intention was to show a truth and explore it.

BLVR: Do you feel like you just have to shut out the audience and the meaning of something as you're kind of figuring out your intentions?

MI: You're communicating with any art, right? I think that the fact that you are communicating means you are aware of an audience. You might not be aware of a demographic or a commercial thing—[or] maybe you are, but the fact that you are thinking about communication with people means you're thinking about an audience.

BLVR: Have audiences with totally different politics from yours changed how you feel about this? I know people took *The Sopranos* to be a lot of glorification.

MI: Yeah, it was very interesting and eye-opening—in a very difficult way, but in a good way. I had just assumed that the audience was all in on it. I'll be really honest with you when I say that David Chase—his intentions, I think, to make this show were much like [those of] Marty Scorsese for *Goodfellas* or Coppola for *The Godfather*. These are great artists who have a connection to these stories and these people based on who they are and where they're from. Yet projecting these images, can we say that it's 100 percent pure and benevolent? I'm not sure, you know what I mean?

I post stuff about gun control because I'm not into guns, whatever—and then people say, *Well, it's hypocritical. You made a lot of money glamorizing gun violence.* I can easily refute that argument in my mind and justify it very effectively. But there's part of me that says, Hmm…

Ultimately, I don't think the intent was to glamorize. The intent was to tell the story.

BLVR: Laurie Anderson's teacher said something that relates for me: practice feeling sad without actually feeling sad. There's value to showing these places and feelings, even if they're dark.

MI: Yeah, you know, there's that word in Sanskrit, *karunā*, like, "that tender heart." When you really open yourself up to others' suffering and things like that, there's a universality to it.

You also have to accept that if you're going to be in samsara, if you're going to make movies, and you're going to be in the public eye, and you're going to have some degree of fame. A desire to make movies—to have the volition to create and do those things—you are creating karma. I'm not necessarily saying negative karma, but you're still in samsara. You're not sliding through the world in this enlightened state that makes no ripple. You know what I mean?

BLVR: Yeah.

MI: I mean, Milarepa, when he decided to go into the mountains and sit in the cave for the rest of his life, basically, I imagine he stopped making ripples.

BLVR: You've talked about how artists need both—to be sensitive people and engage with the world. Maybe the sensitivity is easier.

MI: I guess so.

BLVR: Personally speaking.

MI: There's a wisdom to it. There's a wisdom to sensitivity. It's also your karma to be in the world right now. I mean, I have three kids—they're adults, but I still have some responsibility to them, and a wife, you know. And it's like, I could choose tomorrow to go to Nepal and sit in the cave for the rest of my life. But I have karmic ties. That might be easier, or it may not. But what about these responsibilities?

When the time is right, maybe we'll be in the cave. Hopefully at some point. [*His phone rings.*] I just get a bunch of calls sometimes. It really freaks me out. A bunch of different people call at the same time and it makes me think that something bad has happened.

BLVR: You want to pick it up?

MI: No.

BLVR: [*Laughs*] OK.

MI: I hope nothing bad happens. [*His phone rings.*] See what I mean? [*He picks it up.*] Hello. Hello? Yes. Uh, yeah. I'm in the middle of an interview. I'll see you then.

III. "TAKING MYSELF OUT OF THE EQUATION"

BLVR: You've related the creative process to having a compass and pointing it toward something, being receptive to everything you find. How do you know whether you can trust the compass?

MI: That's a really good question. At the inception of a project—say, if you're an artist, right? Once your consciousness gets tuned to whatever it is—an image, a story, a chord progression, a melody, and you're working on it; you know, it might be a year, not all the time, but you're working on it—once your consciousness gets tuned to that, anything that comes into your head related to that idea, you have to respect it.

You may not use it, but you better write it down. Because at that point there's no random thoughts. Your consciousness—your compass, if you will—is tuned to that. Whatever is coming is filtered through that. You can't ignore any of it. That's how I trust it.

BLVR: Do you ever find that overwhelming?

MI: No, no, I wish. I wish I was overwhelmed by that.

BLVR: Does it feel slow?

MI: No. It's just like: the more the merrier. [*Laughs*]

BLVR: I've felt obsessive about finishing things, but that might just be impatience.

MI: Yeah, there's a fine balance between impatience and the time it needs. At some point you've got to realize that you've got to commit to it—sometimes you just have to start, even if you just have one scene, one image, one moment. Just start playing with it. Sometimes that opens a box. That opens and then there's another one.

BLVR: How do you receive those first ideas?

MI: I think you have to set a space and time for them. If you're writing, especially fiction—that takes a lot of time—that's why you have that daily: All right: Monday through Friday, I'm sitting at the desk, and I'm writing. Whether or not you write a word, it's important to be in that seat. You may not write a word for a whole week. But the mind knows that that time is dedicated to that. Something's going on. If you're going to wait for the inspiration, that's probably going to slow things down.

BLVR: There's that Leonard Cohen line, "Ring the bells that still ring. / Forget your perfect offering." Can't be too precious, even if it's sacred.

MI: Yeah, did you see *Hallelujah*? There's a couple of shots of, like, the notebooks just for "Hallelujah." And there's, like, dozens of them.

BLVR: He did so much work to keep things simple.

MI: Yeah, he was special. He was a spiritual seeker. He definitely got in touch with something.

BLVR: And he's just so raw emotionally. Is that one of the things that draws you to music? You've talked about having a stage presence—the immediate communication you find when you're up there.

MI: Yeah. I really had to figure out how to do that. I really didn't know what the fuck to do. First of all, singing and playing guitar take most of my attention because I'm not so fluent in those things. But once you do find some kind of control, then: Okay. I can actually look at people. I have enough control now that I can look at people—what are you going to say? What are you trying to communicate? People are looking at you. I think now it's really about emotion. Getting inside the story, the song, whatever emotion is evoked.

You're trying to express your energy like an actor does, expressing it in your body as well.

BLVR: Does it feel like playing a character?

MI: It's very, very similar to acting. The song is the script. There's a character but it's not playing a character. It's connecting to it. It's different. Although some of the songs have first-person dialogue. And I've been trying to kind of actually play those characters a little bit. Yeah, that's true. I'm not playing a character as the singer, but within the song, yes.

BLVR: Do you feel like you're doing the Buddhist thing of watching your own mind in those spaces when you're acting or onstage?

MI: I don't know if it's mind looking at mind, because there's so much fixation on what you're doing. [*Laughs*] At least for me at this point.

BLVR: I guess you hear about people who have prepared and done something so much that they're out of body when they're performing.

MI: Like athletes when they have these games. When they're completely in the moment. It's just effortless. I don't think it's the same as mind looking at mind. I think there's a stillness to those moments.

BLVR: Do you think musicians are like religious icons for the culture?

MI: Saying "religion" is a tough one. But when I was a teenager and I first heard the Smiths, Morrissey was very, very, very important to me. For many reasons, but I just felt like he was doing something that not a lot of people were doing. I felt the same thing about David Bowie and Lou Reed. There was an honesty. It was important to me that they were in the world. It made you feel less alone.

BLVR: Is it spiritual?

MI: I felt more like they were teachers. Sometimes the experience of being at a show could be some kind of an ecstatic, transcendent experience, seeing music. If you're seeing somebody that you really connect to, those vibrations—or, you know, again, the molecules—those vibrations are very profound.

BLVR: Is that what happened when you first saw My Bloody Valentine and had to leave?

MI: That was even before the lyrics. I can't even hear them

on the record. But yeah, that's what I hope for every time I go see music. Very often I won't go see music, because I know that's not going to happen. I don't know how to do that intentionally for people beyond, you know, just trying to be honest in the song, committing myself as much as possible.

BLVR: Onstage do you feel something comparable to when you're seeing shows live?

MI: Oh yeah. Even taking myself out of the equation. The sounds that my two bandmates make, being onstage with it, being in sync with it: it's very, very powerful. Those two guys are not just a rhythm section. They're two very distinctive players on their instruments. Olmo is a very powerful drummer. As Elijah is on bass and vocals. You feel a lot. At the times when I get most insecure, I lean on that. The fact that I'm onstage with those two guys gives me confidence, more than I have for myself.

BLVR: Does the noise feel like armor?

MI: Yeah, yeah. But it's also very pleasurable. I like the noise we're making now, but it's a little more specific. It took a while to find the sound. The early stuff is a lot more punk-driven, post-punk. The newer stuff has more psychedelic and shoegaze and indie rock.

BLVR: You're recording more songs now?

MI: Yeah, we just started in August. We did a single last year with John Agnello. We liked it so much we decided to do the album with him. A day opened up, Sunday, and he called a few days ago. He goes, "I'm up here and we've got Sundays open. Do you want to come in?" So we went in. At the studio he works out of in Union City, there's two control rooms. It turned out in the other one was a different producer and the singer Jane Siberry, who we didn't know. He introduced us and we played her the song. She wound up doing some vocals on it, which was a real thrill. I told David Chase and he said, "Well, her song closes *The Many Saints of Newark*." I'd totally forgotten. She was lovely.

BLVR: It seems like chance has played a big part

in growing your community. You wouldn't have started the meditation class if people didn't want it.

MI: Yeah, I think a lot of it's a matter of just being open to it. In Tibetan, there's a word, *tendrel*, which means "auspicious coincidence, auspicious circumstance." So, like, when something happens that seems like a coincidence but it's really very profound, right? Know what I mean? You have to follow those things. It's important to be open to them.

IV. THE GOOD NEWS
(OR: THE WORST THING IN THE WORLD)

BLVR: You get to collaborate a lot when you're screenwriting too.

MI: Although I started *The Perfume Burned His Eyes* because I was sick of collaborating. Not sick of collaborating with people, but there were a lot of projects I loved that I couldn't get going. And I'm like, At least I can do that. I can complete this, whether it gets published or not. It's not like a screenplay or teleplay or a bible for a show where you do it and it never gets made. It's like you didn't really do anything. You know what I mean?

Giving people your unmade screenplays to read, it's fucking the worst thing in the world. At least a novel you can finish.

BLVR: Do you find it easy to take breaks with a novel and go back?

MI: It takes a while. Sometimes it's really good. Sometimes it's not so good. It just is what it is. I wish sometimes that's all I did.

BLVR: Just fiction writing?

MI: Or anything.

BLVR: You want to dig just the one hole a thousand feet deep. Yeah.

MI: Karmically, this is where I'm at right now. There's a bunch of things happening.

BLVR: How do you feel about the watered-down Buddhism that often makes its way into the culture, the kind Mike White's satirized?

MI: It's dangerous or just ineffective. Did you ever read *What Makes You Not a Buddhist*?

BLVR: I haven't.

MI: It's very good. He's a very important teacher right now. He's a filmmaker too. Dzongsar Khyentse Rinpoche. He goes by Khyentse Norbu when he makes films. He's a tulku reincarnate lama from the Khyentse lineage. Really amazing and smart.

BLVR: What are his films like?

MI: *The Cup* is about monks who want to see the World Cup on TV. *Travelers and Magicians* is more about pilgrims. They're interesting films. He understands the West and modernity and artists. He basically says that in the beginning, people want to meditate because they're stressed out. Which is fine, you know, but, he says, if you want to feel better, you're probably better off getting a massage than meditating.

It's not a self-help thing. The goal of Buddhism really is to end delusion from our subjective, human existence. And it demands that we're brutally honest with ourselves. It's a very different trip than most people think Buddhism is, you know?

BLVR: I wanted to ask in your class: How can you be ambitious without being attached?

MI: I don't know if you can. Doing stuff in the world, there's gonna be a certain amount of karma that you're creating. I think part of the challenge is to recognize the attachment. Become aware of it. See that it's there. See how it affects you. How much of it feeds your ego, inflates it, how it affects your expectations and what you're trying to do.

If you can see that, then you really kind of get down to the essence of why you're doing what you're doing. It's also your karma, in a way. You're in this position to do certain things, right? That's who you are.

In Mahayana Buddhism, you take the mind bodhisattva vow, which means: I am committing to return lifetime after lifetime to be of benefit to beings until all beings are enlightened. I'm not going to seek enlightenment just for my own benefit. But I'm going to come back. I'm going to do that until all sentient beings become enlightened.

That's the bodhisattva vow; that's part of the foundation of Mahayana Buddhism. It's a really tall order. It's an easy thing to say the vow, but it's a really big commitment. [*Laughs*] A lot bigger than most of us who take it really know.

BLVR: Nondualism confuses me. I can never really define it or get the idea to stick.

MI: I don't think it ever does. It's not enough to have an intellectual understanding of it. You can, on the level of quantum physics and stuff. But how do you start to bring that into your practice, into your life, and how you engage with the world? I think when you finally realize that and embody it, it becomes your default. That may be Buddhahood. The way we see the world is sort of habituated over lifetimes and in this physical form we are limited to certain sense perceptions, how we perceive the world. There are limits. And a certain functionality you need just to survive comes through duality.

You can go sit in a cave for some kind of release from it. That's a process. There's a teacher, I forget who it was, who said: "Just try not to hurt anybody."

BLVR: I guess the idea being that once you're living all these practices…

MI: If you start to apply awareness to situations, you can bring a positive charge where maybe there would just be a neutral one. Just by your attention and where you're placing it. That's the good news.

BLVR: Do you feel comfortable calling yourself a teacher?

MI: No. Maybe for meditation, but not Buddhism. I can teach meditation. It's very simple, really. Posture, breathing, working with the mind, the techniques. But not Buddhism. I don't know enough to teach that. I mean, that's specific.

BLVR: You chose Tibetan Buddhism because of the teachers.

MI: It's like martial arts, right? All the martial arts have their merits, but it's really about finding the right teacher. That's when you're really going to learn stuff and progress. If you find a teacher that has some realization and is from an authentic lineage, you should leap. They're as rare as stars in the daytime, as they say. ✶

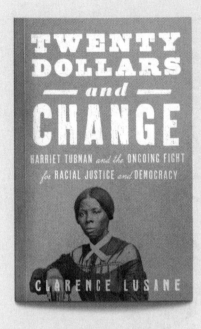
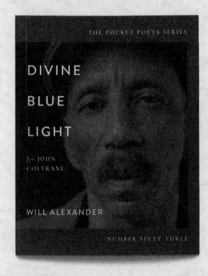
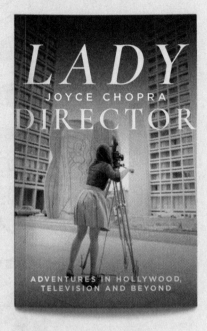

Considering the rarely discussed, highly stigmatized experience that touches almost every writer's career: the failed book

The CURSE of KAFKA

by **ANDREA BAJANI**; *translated by Elizabeth Harris*   *illustrations by* **KYLE HILTON**

What is the point of saving such "even" artistically misbegotten works? Because one hopes that these fragments will somehow combine to form from my whole, some court of appeals upon whose breast I shall be able to throw myself when I am in need?

—Franz Kafka to Max Brod
[Prague, end of December 1917]

1.

or a few months, about ten years back, I regularly went to the liver transplant unit of a hospital in Turin, where I lived at the time. I'd take my bike, sail past the train tracks, and ten minutes later I'd slip my bike into the rack, among all the others. Then I'd step through the hospital's sliding-glass doors. My bike would stay out there in that thicket of frames, wheels, and chains, along with the bicycles of doctors, nurses, and patients.

I took the elevator from the main floor, and at the third ding, I'd step out and walk to Surgery 2. Sometimes I knocked; other times the doctor was already waiting for me by the door in his white coat. He'd shake my hand and whisk me into his office. I rarely had to wait long in that hallway, that place of transit where a person's complexion, the gurney going by, the tone of the voices indicated the treatment of a body, and hope or despair.

Only once did the surgeon not show up, and after an hour, I asked a nurse what was happening. Two emergency surgeries in a row, she said, and now maybe a third. She didn't know when he'd be available, probably not before that evening.

I sent him an email the next day, and he suggested I come back the following week. Two livers had arrived, he told me across his desk when I was there again. Which meant the following process: preparing operating tables, surgeons, nurses. And the relay race of life and death connected to all this— a human being had died, and another human being, as a direct result of this death, would be saved.

A helicopter took off with the liver just explanted from the body, the phones of three sick people started ringing, and then three families in three different parts of Italy hopped into their cars and raced to the hospital, each with a bag of clean clothes.

Of those three families, only one stayed in the hospital and started a new life with the horizon, finally, in the distance. Two families returned home a few hours later with the same battered liver from before, the sick still just as sick. They were the families in reserve, and they knew it: the liver wasn't for them unless complications arose during surgery.

When I sat down across from him, the doctor didn't give me all these details. He said only that two organs had arrived, and that's why we had to postpone our meeting. The rest— the relay between life and death—was implied; his job was to make it happen. Then he said: "So let's continue."

2A.

I'd begun meeting with the surgeon because I wanted to write a novel about organ transplants. All it took was an email. His human curiosity and shared passion for books did the rest.

"Why are you so interested in transplants?" he asked the first time we met. I told him I didn't know— no specific reason. "A sick relative?" No, no one.

The only incident I recalled was from twenty years before. I had driven my first girlfriend, S., to the hospital in Cuneo because while we were out, she'd received a breathless phone call from her mother. Her father had been notified that a liver was available. They'd been waiting awhile—my girlfriend needed to go to the hospital at once. I was eighteen years old and had just gotten my license, and what I remember most about that episode was the tension of driving her there, and the pride I felt for the decisive role I played in something so serious.

My girlfriend's father recovered quickly, and he returned to a relatively normal life. He ran a paper manufacturing company and had a son who would succeed him but was still too young at the time. So after the father's hospital stay, and by taking his daily pills (I remembered those pills, and that his sentence, so to speak, was to take them for life), he was doing all right fairly soon. I'd gone to visit him at his home after the operation, as this seemed like the natural thing to do. His daughter and I felt we were destined to marry, for the simple reason that it never occurred to either of us that we might break up.

He got back to working at full tilt, just as energetic and persistent as before. But his daughter and I did break up a year later, for no other reason than we'd gotten older. That's why we stayed friends, and continued to have sex, out of attraction and because our bodies belonged together, would always belong together. Or so we thought. Then we lost track of each other, which was only natural. Years later, she wrote to me that her father's liver had been rejected, and they'd operated again. He had a new one, and was back to being a lion.

Was that why I wanted to write a book about transplants? I told the surgeon I didn't think so. Before he asked, I hadn't remembered this at all. It might just be a hunch, I said, but maybe if we all knew more about transplants, if we understood them a little more, the world would be better off. And maybe we'd understand the politics of immigration, understand gang violence, even shyness, if only we could learn how each of our bodies would react when something foreign, an organ, was removed from them and inserted—forced, really—into someone else's space.

2B.
TO MAX BROD
[MATLIARY, SECOND HALF
OF JANUARY 1921]

Dearest Max,
Another postscript, so that you can see how the Enemy proceeds…. Here torture goes on for years, with pauses for effect so that it will not go too quickly and— the unique element—the victim himself is compelled, by his own will, out of his own wretched inner self, to protract the torture. This whole wretched life in bed, the fever, the shortness of breath, the taking of medicines, the painful and dangerous business with the mirrors (one little awkward motion and he can burn himself)—all this has no other purpose but to slow down the development of the abscesses from which he must finally suffocate, to prolong this wretched life, the fever and so on, as long as possible. And his relatives and the doctors and visitors have literally built some scaffoldings over this not burning but slowly smoldering pyre, so that without danger of contagion they can visit, cool, and comfort the tormented man, cheer him up to endure further misery.

3A.

During the time I was visiting the surgeon, I had just begun a new relationship. My decade-long love affair was crumbling, and then one January night, it ended in a moment of apnea. After two years of indecision, fighting, astronomical distances in bed, I came to a halt while doing laps in a pool. I couldn't breathe. The lifeguard shouted to me, leaned over the water, wanting to know if I needed any help. I waved him off, then dragged myself to the end of the pool, then to the locker room, then into the car and home. Four days later, a van came for M.'s boxes and her few pieces of furniture.

My early notes for the transplant novel coincided with the beginning of a new love. After M. left, the apartment felt abandoned, with all its visible subtractions: the missing paintings, the chasm of an absent desk beneath the window. Unable to revive the place, I let it die. I moved into the small apartment with a balcony where E. and her twelve-year-old daughter lived. I couldn't bring myself to get my life back in order, and so I wound up embedded in someone else's already perfectly organized life.

In spite of the minimal space and that intimate, absolute coexistence of daughter and mother, they made room for me with a kind of cheerfulness. The daughter, watchful; the mother, solicitous on two fronts, her every gesture protective of her daughter and of me—two castaways beached on the sixth floor. And at the same time she was giving herself and her daughter— the two of them—the chance to reconstruct something resembling a family.

So the first notes on transplants were from that period. The beginnings of a novel? I don't know—I don't think so. I was working to finish a different book, which had been frozen for too long and would ultimately end in apnea, along with my previous relationship. The main character of that novel had gone to Russia to learn more about his grandfather, who'd fought on the Russian front, on the Ukrainian border, in the ranks of the fascist army, and had then gone mad when he returned to a life of peace. For over a year, I couldn't get him off the steppe;

whenever I opened my laptop I found him there, frozen, lacking the courage to go home. My new love—my new life within an already functioning, prearranged life—helped me bring this book to a close, as though love and writing were directly linked. Both could exist only if you could see the horizon from somewhere, the promise of a future. My main character would meet a young woman with a baby girl, and everything would be set back in motion. He'd return to Italy, fly from 1943 to the present, landing in 2010.

At the same time, or immediately after, I began jotting down my thoughts on transplants. I started going to the hospital and meeting with the surgeon, developed an interest in physiology, bought and read medical manuals, which I have to admit I didn't fully understand.

The surgeon was patient with me. More than once a doctor or nurse interrupted us. He'd stop, answer their questions, then go back to our conversation.

One day we heard someone knock, a couple with two children; I caught a glimpse of them through the crack of the door. The surgeon stepped out, and when he returned, he told me this happened quite a bit, that patients' families would come to thank him. They brought gifts, bottles of wine, flowers. He had a room full of ex-votive offerings. He'd restored their loved one's life, and they wanted to show him they were grateful.

He wouldn't accept any gifts before the outcome of the surgery was clear. Those gifts held too much desperate hope. If there were postoperative complications—if the organ didn't feel at home, so to speak, in its new body—relatives might hold him accountable. What if the transplanted organ were to rebel, if it turned against the body it was supposed to save, even threatened to kill the patient? Then the family could say: *You take our gifts, and then our son dies like that?*

I often asked myself why the doctor was willing to answer my questions. What were his reasons? Why did my questions matter to him? One day, he told me the point was to want to live, to want to live at all costs. Or not. "Perhaps that's of interest to you," he said. Before authorizing a transplant, he said, the so-called "candidates" underwent interviews with a team of psychologists and doctors. The people who wanted to live at all costs—you could tell right away, he said, just by hearing them speak—those people would survive. The ones who didn't really want to wouldn't make it. There were people who were clinically compromised, who wound up with a bad

organ, too, and they'd go on to live another twenty years. You could tell it in the interviews—they wanted to live, and they *would* live, even without a heart. And then there were others, in better shape, who didn't make it.

Was this, he wondered, what tied writing to his profession? Creating the conditions, the habitat, for a man or woman to be able to survive in a hostile environment? And who was it, he asked me, who survived in the writing—the characters? The author, I said, poking myself in the chest. I was the one trying to survive in a hostile environment (life), and I needed a transplant of artificial life (a story) to be able to go on a little longer.

3B.
TO MAX BROD [MATLIARY, END OF MAY/BEGINNING OF JUNE 1921]

This by and large out-of-the-world life which I lead here is not in itself worse than any other. I have no reason to complain about it. But if the world shouts a ghoulish cry into my gravelike peace, then I fly off the handle and beat my forehead against the door of madness which is always unlatched.

4A.

I worked on the book in waves for a couple of years. I kept taking notes, wrote a few pages, met other doctors. I also took an interest in plant grafting, but then abandoned this—it felt unproductive. But I never abandoned the project.

In the meantime, my old home—the one I'd shared with M.—died entirely, and we made a new one. We moved my furniture and E.'s into an empty apartment, and we started a new life, all three of us. We started from scratch, the two of them plus me. We put a single last name by the intercom to make us a real family. We got married, and it was a happy marriage. We took more family photos than couple photos, because this was the heart of the matter. Taking the broken pieces and building something complete.

The years went by. We made plans and promises every day, partly out of love, partly for upkeep. We moved to Berlin, took more family photos. One day, in a restaurant, a waiter told us E.'s daughter looked like me, though we had no genes in common. E. and I felt proud of ourselves: we'd made it—our artificial family had become a natural one.

But I couldn't write anymore; the transplant novel hadn't even begun and had already shut down on me. At home, tensions grew. I started to step aside, to keep to myself. To think in terms of "me" and "them." If they were both home, I went out. I could feel the hostility radiating from E.'s daughter. Or was it me who was hostile? I couldn't say, but I do know that little by little everything was going back to how it started: they were the family; I was the transplanted organ, inserted into the body of another. We made an emergency move from Berlin back to Turin; we were on the brink of collapse.

During that time, my transplant novel started to die a painful death. I'd try to write, but the words were lifeless. I spent my days in my office, filling up pages with sterile sentences. I kept tapping away on my keyboard, but it was all useless. I was home less and less. The crisis had seemingly blown over. But I still felt like a foreign body in that family, in the generations of Turin's Catholic bourgeoisie that E. belonged to. Shut up in my office, seven minutes from home, I'd ask words to provide me with a different life—but what life?

Then my novel died outright. I noted this one evening; there was nothing left to be done. I saved it on my laptop, in my "Incomplete" folder, my small graveyard of unfinished books. I wrote the final date, January 21, 2015. I went back home, sat down at the table; we ate in silence. A few hours later, in bed, when E.'s breathing grew heavy, I let myself fall into despair. I hugged her from behind. In her sleep, E. stroked my arm, while I soaked her back with tears. Then I loosened my hold and dissolved into dreams.

I never reopened that file, not until recently, as I started to write this. The last note was a dialogue with the surgeon, and afterward, the definitive white silence of abandonment. As written:

> ME: Doctor, I'm not interested in metaphors. I want to understand how a transplant works, the mechanics of it. What happens when a foreign organ is inserted into a new body?
>
> DOCTOR: That body tries to destroy it.
>
> ME: And how do you keep it from being destroyed?
>
> DOCTOR: By administering an immunosuppressant—an anti-rejection pill.
>
> ME: So the body will stop trying to destroy the organ?

MICROINTERVIEW WITH WO CHAN, PART III

THE BELIEVER: Your poetry and drag seem to have evolved and grown alongside each other. I'm especially interested in how you've used the screen in drag performances, projecting text behind you.

WO CHAN: Yes! This is kind of a joke, but I love being introduced as the progenitor of PowerPoint drag. You know how in poetry school people say that every line should be strong enough to be the title? I think about that when I set up slides: every slide should be strong enough that if someone takes a picture of it, it should have some kind of resonance. So it's never just me standing in front of a PowerPoint that says the word *and*, right? That doesn't really do anything. It has to be a phrase that interacts with my body. Combining poetry with drag has given me a way to express nuance beyond the limitations of my body. Some people are flexible; some people can do cartwheels; some people just have a wider range of physical expression. So I realized I could bring my poetic strengths to the drag scene, which is of course already so interdisciplinary. ✴

DOCTOR: No, the pill is only a peacemaker. The body will always try to destroy the organ. The organ is—will always be—the enemy. An unwelcome guest.

4B.
[FRANZ KAFKA'S DIARIES, NOVEMBER 30, 1914]

I can't write any more. I've come up against the last boundary, before which I shall in all likelihood... begin another story all over again that will again remain unfinished. This fate pursues me.

5.

The graveyard of books I've never finished takes up 38.8 megabytes on my desktop. All the projects I've never brought to a close. As I'm writing this, six novels lie in that small digital graveyard. Some are only a few pages of notes, fragments, passages of dialogue. Or photographs, images, web links to check, audio files. Others have dozens of pages that waited awhile for others to arrive, but they never did. At a certain point, the writing just stopped, came to a standstill in the nothing of the page.

Simply put, there came a point when the novel was gone. The words stopped. And my every attempt to bring the text back to life, to make it breathe through my sentences, was pointless. The novel had gone out. All that preparation, of characters, events, travels, actions, dialogue, toward some final design, ended in a desert of meaning. Men and women had nothing more to say, to tell one another. There were no more trips they wanted to take. No more consoling gestures, no more actions producing reactions that could make a man or a woman get up off a chair. No questions demanded answers. No one wanted anything more. Everything ended in surrender. White flag, white page.

I'd just sit staring at my screen. I talked about it with friends, asked for help. All they said was "Think about Kafka—he almost never finished anything." And then they'd change the subject because there was nothing more to say. "Yeah? Well, why didn't he?" And they didn't know, and I didn't know, and no one knew. And the conversation had already moved on.

That unconditional surrender of things and people was too lifelike not to hurt. Didn't I write because life wasn't enough—so I could at least force life into the meaning of a sentence? Didn't I write because I couldn't seem to accept that everything I said and did had no direction other than the senselessness of endlessly doing something? What was I doing with my life—my memories, my pain, even my happiness—if I couldn't at least shape it into a story?

I'm a disciplined writer, a strong-willed writer. Every morning, I get up before dawn and sit down at the table with a cup of coffee. I'm convinced that positioning myself so close to the end of sleep leaves the door open for dreams. That from there, from the table where I've sat down with my hands just above the keyboard, I can see dreams, can tap into the primordial chaos of dream life while staying on dry ground in my ordinary reality. My cup of coffee, the hum of the refrigerator, the feel of the cold floor beneath my feet. In short, I'm convinced that the source of writing—even more than the stories—is an exact point, a precise time between the end of night and the start of day. A fragile space that vanishes in an instant, leaving nothing more to say.

To achieve this, I've always written in the kitchen. Because it's here that I can see dreams better while still grasping hold of life. Every time I've tried to set up an office over the years, to furnish a space where I can write, it hasn't worked out. My words have never come to life there. Every time, after getting that "writing room" ready, after setting my desk the proper distance from the window, putting the proper books on the shelves for the proper landscape to write in, then sitting down at the proper time of day—every time, I've then moved to the kitchen. And it's there, among the leftover bread crumbs from dinner, the tablecloth pushed to one side, that the words have reappeared, famished, hungering after those crumbs.

And the office has been left for photos, when photographers would come by and want me to pose as a writer. "Stand in there," they'd say. "It's the perfect shot, with that view, the buildings out front, the trees, Pasolini's books behind you, your notebook, your Parker pen lying on top."

Over time, I gave up on having an office. My writing method seemed infallible: in the kitchen, with the door open to dreams. I just needed to stop when the garbage trucks arrived. They were easy to hear, with their relentless accelerating and braking, and then the crash of empty dumpsters, the mechanical arm dropping them on the sidewalk. These trucks were my allies; I relied on the complicity of the garbagemen, on the garbage brigade. Their process that told me: *Time to leave—fall back, everyone's holding life to account now.*

I always trusted this. When I heard the dumpsters hit the asphalt, I stopped writing. And yet, in spite of my well-tested method, at a certain point, some novels just died on me. But why? It was the right time: the kitchen supplied the reality, sleep brought on dreams. Yet words refused to appear, to step onto the screen. *Where are you?* I felt like shouting at them in that nothingness. *Why have you abandoned me? Why are you condemning me to silence?*

And I'd end up sitting there in the kitchen, waiting for the garbage trucks and their relentless call. Hoping they'd come as soon as possible. *Please, garbagemen, please have mercy on me. Please let me stop.*

And when I finally heard them, I'd shut my laptop and raise my hands in surrender.

6A.

I've always tried to avert the premature death of my books. I've tried in every possible way to escape what my friends called "the curse of Kafka." Kafka, the abandoner par excellence. The man of unfinished novels. I've always thought that at least he, Kafka, had the answer as to why one didn't finish after having begun something. Up to the very end of his life, he kept on not finishing. And wasn't asking his most trusted friend, Max Brod, to burn everything or nearly everything he'd ever written—wasn't this, too, perhaps eliminating that final

close, that last ending, which death, as it comes, fixes in place?

I even sought help from geography, trying to remove myself physically from that curse. Not being home seemed like an option. This is why I've traveled a great deal. I've hidden in other people's homes to overcome the curse of Kafka. I've written in Genoa, Paris, Amsterdam, Hamburg, Montpellier, Bucharest, Moscow, Lisbon. There's an entire world map of my absence from home, an escape route, a way out.

Sometimes it worked. Other times, relentless Kafka came knocking at the door.

6B.

TO MAX BROD [BERLIN-STEGLITZ; POSTMARKED ON ARRIVAL: OCTOBER 25, 1923]

So if I do not write, that is due chiefly to "strategic" reasons such as have become dominant for me in recent years. I do not trust words and letters, my words and letters; I want to share my heart with people but not with phantoms that play with the words and read the letters with slavering tongue.

7A.

On March 4, 2016, I decided to stop writing, or at least to stop trying so hard. If a novel came pounding down the door of the page, I'd let it in. Otherwise, I didn't find it all that important to try. Thanks—but no.

Up to that moment, I'd structured my life around a living-writing binomial, and I never thought it could be otherwise. What would I do with my life if I didn't glean details from it that I turned into a story? What would I do with myself if I had to wait for the final

ending, death, to make sense of every day I had lived?

Becoming a so-called professional writer was natural for me, yet in a way, this couldn't have been a greater miscalculation on my part. It meant turning my search for meaning into a career, for profit. Writing even to pay the rent. Writing for a living became true in every sense. If I didn't write, I wouldn't eat, and if I didn't write, I'd go crazy.

So I automatically (so to speak) became a writer by trade. I took the easiest path, occupied my place within a crowded world already set up for this. All it took was one well-received novel to get the ball rolling. I began a routine that was largely standard by the 2000s. There were so many of us with the same ambition. I started writing for newspapers. First reviews, then regular columns. Traveling, reporting, trains, airplanes. Rarely at home: my rhythms dictated by packing and unpacking my suitcase.

Literary festivals, reviews, book tours, on beaches or in the mountains during the summer, bookstores, theaters, schools, breathtaking landscapes with the author, author cocktail hours, author dinners. Whenever I arrived, I'd take possession of my hotel room, climb up onto a stage. Talk, applause, get off the stage. Go to a dinner, talk, eat, return to my hotel, sleep.

Posing for photos was a corollary of this trade, and it was inevitable. I started even before I was thirty, learning to pose, to look at a distant point just over the photographer's shoulder, and to set my gaze in the only manner possible, a writerly one. There were so many of us, our photos all alike. Drawn-out gaze, expansive thoughts, so sweeping. And then the photo on the page beside the interview, or on the poster. Because the writer knows. Knows more. *Writer, tell us something wise. Writer, make us laugh. Or cry.* And I'd say something wise, or funny, or moving.

The morning after, in the hotel, I'd wake up feeling so sad, I'd be choking on it. Meaninglessness was sitting there at the foot of my bed, staring me in the face.

Through this inordinate miscalculation, I surrendered to a ceaseless search for meaning. It was my trade. Receiving applause, someone waiting at the train station, the airport. "Good afternoon, Mr. Bajani. Welcome," from a well-dressed concierge in a hotel I could never have allowed myself in the past. Being interviewed, saying something meaningful and not saying it alone, having a public, thinking of it as a community. Wasn't this the end of loneliness? Wasn't this the compensation I deserved?

Except in order to keep having this, I had to keep writing. If I didn't write, the light went out. The carriage turned back into a pumpkin. So I began to torment myself with words, to flay myself for a story, so I could earn a bit of meaning.

And I looked at the photos they were taking of me. Leaning against a tree, bucolic gaze. A defunct factory behind me, the postindustrial writer. Or thoughtful, in the same pose as every other writer on earth, hand beneath my chin. And the more I looked at those photos, the more I thought, What does that person have to do with me? What does he have to do with that twenty-year-old boy who tore out his own beard, pulled chunks of flesh from his own face, because physical pain was the only way not to feel the hurt inside? Who rode his Vespa for hours alone, out in the countryside, because the noise of the motor silenced the buzzing of his thoughts? What did the writer in that photo have to do with the boy trying to find some respite from domestic violence, from a father's fury, a man who'd decided not to live in his own hell but to drag his wife and two children down with him?

What did that luxury hotel, that "Good afternoon, Mr. Bajani," have to do with that boy tapping on a keyboard, trying to find some peace inside a sentence? What did applause have to do with a boy who was uncertain how to live, and how this moved his hands over the page, dividing his pain into lines of poetry? And the cocktail hours, the literary festivals, those snacks of meaning offered like peanuts along with a spritz, for an hour with a sea view? Come one, come all, take your seat, snack on this guy, too, and he'll help you live a better life.

And me, climbing up, and all of us, climbing up, considering our look before it's offered, clearing our throats before we speak, preparing to see the effect our voices have on others. Speaking, declaring, shaping our sentences, looking for approval, for applause.

7B.
[KAFKA'S DIARIES, JANUARY 24, 1922]

Hesitation before birth. If there is a transmigration of souls then I am not yet on the bottom rung. My life is a hesitation before birth.

8A.

I decided to quit writing while I was staying at a baroque villa on the Regnitz River in Bavaria. For eleven months, twelve of us—writers, composers, and artists—were to live in an austere but charming villa in the historic center of Bamberg. The city of nearly eighty thousand is one of the tourist centers of Franconia, a German region known for its wine and its hills. The historic center is one of the few the 1945 British and American bombing raids didn't destroy. The river runs through this center, the sunset painting purple evenings on the water.

At the entrance to the villa, our twelve names had been painted on the steps, announcing to the citizens of Bamberg and to passing tourists: *Inside are twelve artists. Beyond this door, artists are creating, letting their imaginations roam. For an entire year they'll write novels, compose sonatas, paint masterpieces.*

Periodically, the villa was open to the public. About once a month, in the afternoon, the front door opened, and men and women stomped on our names and took their seats in the performance hall. One by one, each of us would climb onto the stage and give an account of our work to the townspeople. *Here's what we're doing in here*, we'd say. *Here is our trade.*

Except that for eleven months, I didn't write a single line. I'd get up early every morning, open the window overlooking the river, turn on my computer, and sit staring at the screen, waiting for a sentence to make an appearance. When the morning was over, if no sentence had arrived, I'd close my laptop and walk along the river until I was exhausted. If there was a sentence, I'd delete it.

I'd taken a lot of notes before coming to Bamberg. I'd even written a story three years before, for a Roman literary festival that I thought would work as the first chapter for the book I wanted to write. A novel titled "The Forgiveness Machine." The same title as the story. For three years, I'd tried to write this and failed.

I'd read a magazine article about the American artist Karen Green and her installation *The Forgiveness Machine*. In 2009, in a gallery in South Pasadena, California, Karen Green had exhibited an actual machine that was more like a giant toy, designed to forgive. Visitors were invited to write down on a piece of paper what they were seeking to forgive—a person, an action. The machine took the piece of paper and pulverized it into a final

snow at rest. Pulverized, the words, the name, brought forgiveness. And, finally, some peace.

What struck me, though, wasn't so much the peace following this forgiveness, but its reverse. Some people (I read in an interview), about to slip the piece of paper into the machine, paused. They couldn't do it. That toy, a supposed game, was suddenly serious. What then? they wondered. What then—what would become of me if I actually forgave this person?

Reading that article, I was paralyzed. Renouncing the crumbling of words in the name of forgiveness, those people were saying: *And what will become of me if I renounce my enemy? Forgiving him, renouncing my enemy, means renouncing a reason, albeit an antagonistic one, to live. Can I be without him or her? Can I truly exist in peace, survive without saying,* It's all his fault? That's what the visitors to the gallery in South Pasadena seemed to be saying, those who'd

---

BOOKS AND POEMS READ IN DONNA TARTT'S *THE SECRET HISTORY*

★ *The Republic*, Book II by Plato
★ *Paradise Lost* by John Milton
★ *Agamemnon* by Aeschylus
★ *The Oresteia* by Aeschylus
★ *Poetics* by Aristotle
★ *The Iliad* by Homer
★ *The Bacchae* by Euripides
★ *Parmenides* by Plato
★ *The Great Gatsby* by F. Scott Fitzgerald
★ *Ivanhoe* by Sir Walter Scott
★ "The Waste Land" by T. S. Eliot
★ *The Adventures of Sherlock Holmes* by Sir Arthur Conan Doyle
★ *Madame Bovary* by Gustave Flaubert
★ *Vanity Fair* by William Makepeace Thackeray
★ *Othello* by William Shakespeare
★ *The Invisible Man* by H. G. Wells
★ *Peter Pan, or The Boy Who Wouldn't Grow Up* by J. M. Barrie
★ *The Divine Comedy* by Dante
★ *The Upanishads*
★ "Lycidas" by John Milton
★ *Doctor Faustus* by Christopher Marlowe
★ *The Revenger's Tragedy* by Cyril Tourneur
★ *Our Mutual Friend* by Charles Dickens

—*list compiled by Eliza Browning*

decided against inserting a word, a name, a sentence, into the machine. *Can I do it?*

Living without an enemy—that was the point. After I read an interview with Karen Green in a women's weekly magazine, I thought about my father. His life, and consequently ours, had been a constant hunt for the enemy. Every person connected to our family had systematically fallen victim to that skeet shooting. Hadn't we all been paralyzed by the terror of his obsessive search for the enemy? Didn't his every threat—screams, smashed objects, wall punches—hold the same allusion: Maybe you want to become my enemy too? Relatives, friends, first they'd appear, and then they were entered into the registry of enemies. And suddenly they disappeared, never to be mentioned again. Grandparents, aunts and uncles, work colleagues. Poof—gone. If we—my mother, my sister, or I—ever mentioned them, we might end up on that list as well. No abatement, no pity. A scream, then silence.

For eleven months, looking out on the Regnitz River, I wasn't able to write a single line. I re-read Karen Green interviews, searched for information online, other photographs of the installation. I tried to create a chorus of pardoners and a chorus of executioners. I did interviews, took photographs.

But none of this ever became a story. At night I'd see the lights on late in the others' rooms. I'd catch sight of the writers behind their curtains, silhouettes huddled over keyboards. In the darkness of my room, I'd curse them, curse myself, curse writing.

A photographer came to take pictures of me in my Bavarian room. I wore a nice shirt, raised my hands over the keyboard, pretended to write. He snapped the photo. I changed clothes, put on a T-shirt, and we went someplace else. He snapped another photo.

I made one last, desperate attempt. I'd record what I had to say. If the words wouldn't come from my hands, maybe they'd come from my mouth. Every morning for a month, I'd go down to the baroque villa's basement with my digital voice recorder. Every morning, when the recorder's red light went on, I'd start talking. I spoke slowly, searching for the right words, forming the sentences in my mind. Morning after morning, I said everything I had to say. At the end of each session, exhausted, I'd return to my room, and sleep for two hours. Extracting words from my body was brutal, tearing them from my flesh. And it was useless—the body holds no words.

After a month, I was done; I saved hours of my voice on my laptop. I tried to listen to myself. I turned myself off. I tried to transcribe my voice. I re-read what I'd transcribed. The delirium of a desperate man—it had nothing to do with literature.

At the end of my residency, I thanked the director and her staff for inviting me. I said the past eleven months had been crucial, because I'd decided to stop writing. I'm not so sure they considered this to be such a great outcome—here was a place designed to support writers in their writing—but they couldn't help but hear my gratitude, and I their affection, their professional esteem, and their compassion.

Before leaving my room on the Regnitz, I wrote all the organizers of the literary festivals who'd invited me to present my books in the following months. I apologized, but I couldn't do it anymore. I canceled every event. And I asked my publishing house not to schedule any more.

I took one last trip to Nuremberg, a half-hour train ride from Bamberg. I walked down the stairs of the villa and stepped on my name. I took the local train. I walked in Nuremberg's historic center for a few hours. I ordered a beer, ate some currywurst. I returned to Bamberg and packed my bags to leave forever. I was free.

8B.
TO MAX BROD [PLANÁ, POSTMARKED ON ARRIVAL: SEPTEMBER 11, 1922]

Fundamentally, loneliness is my sole aim, my greatest temptation, my opportunity, and assuming it can be said that I have "arranged" my life, it was always with the view that loneliness can comfortably fit into it.

9A.

More than seven years have passed since that March day in 2016 when I walked out the imposing front door of the Villa Concordia in Bamberg. Since then, I've stopped thinking about the small graveyard of my unfinished books. Or at least I've stopped doing it with the same tortuous hope as before, when knocking on the door of a failed book meant contemplating—anticipating?—that one way or another, someone would eventually open that door for me, and I could bring the book back to life.

Since then, my periodic visits have only been commemorative, for appeasement's sake. A ritualistic gesture, a walk among the headstones, a changing of the flowers. That much was necessary, a polite gesture, honoring the dead.

I've opened the folder on my desktop, made sure everything was in its place. "The Forgiveness Machine"

EVERY INSTANCE IN WHICH JANE EYRE CALLS MR. ROCHESTER "UGLY" IN *JANE EYRE* BY CHARLOTTE BRONTË (IN ORDER)

* "Had he been a handsome, heroic-looking young gentleman, I should not have dared to stand thus questioning him against his will, and offering my services unasked. I had hardly ever seen a handsome youth."
* "More remarkable for character than beauty."
* "Neither tall nor graceful."
* "Do you think me handsome?"
  "No, sir.'"
* "[Mr. Rochester's forehead] showed a solid enough mass of intellectual organs, but an abrupt deficiency where the suave sign of benevolence should have risen."
* "His unusual breadth of chest, disproportionate almost to his length of limb. I am sure most people would have thought him an ugly man."
* "The lack of mere personal attractiveness."
* "Imperfect."
* "Harsh to inferiority."
* "My master's colourless, olive face, square, massive brow, broad and jetty eyebrows, deep eyes, strong features, firm, grim mouth,—all energy, decision, will,—were not beautiful."
* "He was rather an ugly man, but quite a gentleman."
* "Harsh-featured and melancholy-looking."
* "It would be past the power of magic, sir [to make Mr. Rochester a handsome man]."
* "His whole face was colourless rock."
* "Acrid and desolate."
* "Alarming."
* "A brownie."
* "Am I hideous, Jane?"
  "Very, sir: you always were, you know."
* "His countenance reminded one of a lamp quenched, waiting to be relit."
* "Vulcan."

—list compiled by Emily Lang

(2013–2016), "The Book of Transplants" (2010–2015). Another novel, untitled (2014–2015), focusing on a local pharmacy in Rome, the broken dream of a pharmacist from southern Italy, from Puglia, ruined by debt in the era of Big Pharma. Another novel, untitled (2009–2010), a lot of notes and not much writing, a sort of biography of Stalin's son who committed suicide, or so they say, because his father disowned and publicly humiliated him. Detained in a Nazi concentration camp in Oranienburg, on April 14, 1943, he fled toward the electrified barbed wire, knowing how it would end, in machine gun fire. Then there was "The Persecution of the Doppelgänger" (2007–2008), the story of a man's persecution, for the sole reason that this man resembled his persecutor's worst enemy.

Then, finally, a novel from an earlier time, untitled (2005–2007), my first real failure. The main character was a boy who loved hockey and whose father worked with businesses that had gone bankrupt. Almost every afternoon, the father brought the boy with him to do inventories of the businesses that had shut down, the employees having abandoned the buildings on the spot, without warning.

The father and son spent hours like this, in bombed-out landscapes, everything left as it was before the owner's announcement that the company had gone bankrupt. Pens lying across paper, children's photos sitting on desks, barrettes clipped to drawer handles.

The father would list what he saw in monotone, and the boy wrote it all down on a notepad. Then the father would come up with a sum, an

economic value of that jumble of failed things.

Afternoons went on like this, in deserted hangars, exterminated by things. Often, rats had gnawed their way into the vending machines.

The novel—with the working title "The Book of Failures"—was set in the winter. Snow everywhere, outside the buildings. And freezing inside, because like everything else, the electricity had been cut off. The father and boy slowly went from room to room, two clouds rising from their mouths.

The boy couldn't stand his father, perhaps due to his age, or his pent-up anger. One day during a fight, he'd shouted that his father was nothing but a gravedigger making money off others' misfortunes.

At night, the boy would pull on his skates, his hockey pads and helmet, and get on the ice. Here, grace, speed, and violence intertwined. The boy was unbeatable in that dance on blades. But it always ended in a fight. The boy would yank off his gloves, hit someone bare-fisted, hurt him. And get ejected, every time.

The father would watch, and feel troubled. But he never commented. The next afternoon, he'd take the boy with him to do more inventories. There was a silence between them that was hard to decipher. There was also a care to the father's work that moved me as I wrote. And that legacy, the dignity, even, of giving value to what had failed—this perhaps was something that neither of them could understand.

Since my German residency, since March 2016, every time I poke my head inside that graveyard of failed novels, I do so with affection rather than frustration. And even now, as I'm writing this, there seems to be some kind of justice—beauty—to this gesture of mine, this writing. Giving value to what has failed.

As I type these pages on my computer on an early summer morning, I feel I'm wandering around inside those desolate, bombed-out hangars. Except there aren't any pens lying across paper, no pictures of sons and daughters in silver frames—just these stories left unfinished, gone bankrupt for reasons that will always remain a mystery. Pharmacists, persecutors, the forgiven and the forgivers, surgeons, patients, young hockey players, they'll just stay put, their gestures never fully making sense.

Now that I'm doing this inventory of my own, it feels like there's a reason for all this senselessness. Simply, that it, too, has a right to citizenship. It's not a graveyard but a habitat, a microclimate, the only place possible for these missing stories to survive, to live together, without

having to apologize for not being able to end. Living like everybody else, with extreme effort, sentences unfinished, gestures unrealized, caresses ungiven.

Don't I, after all, teach my students about the relationship that exists between inventory and invention? Don't I tell them every day that there's no vision other than what arises from taking stock, from the inventory, the list of what remains? That inventing is nothing but sitting there, just like a father and son inside an ice-cold building, and pronouncing, in monotone, all the life remaining on the table, after the end has dropped like an ax? That you have to be brave when you write and hold only half-lives in your hands?

9B.
[NOTE WRITTEN BY FRANZ KAFKA, KIERLING SANATORIUM]

Here it is nice to give… because everyone is a little bit of a connoisseur, after all.

10.

Since March 2016, the graveyard of my unfinished books has stayed exactly the same. For seven years, no other text that hoped to be a book has gone inside. It's just stayed there, like a parallel bibliography to the novels— in the midst of those failed attempts— that I managed to finish. Would I have written those novels that I published without those others that failed? I don't know. It doesn't matter—what matters is that those failures have a place to stay.

My marriage to E. didn't survive my German residency. You might say it didn't survive my exit from writing. I tried to prop it up, using sentences as permanent scaffolding. As long as

I kept trying to write sentences—no matter how clumsy—to keep us inside a story, the relationship could endure. But the moment I let go of writing, I had to come to terms with what I still held in my grasp. I had to take stock, an inventory. "What happens, doctor, when an organ's transplanted into a different body?" That body tries to destroy it, and will always try, until the very end. The surgeon had said this, but it never made it into a story; it happened only in life.

Our marriage ended like many marriages, with a courtroom, rage, pain, and the division of assets, reasons, and faults. This happened to us, too, one September morning in 2018. First we said our names before a judge, and then we left, bruised with hostility and pain, and walked back to our bikes. And we went our separate ways, leaving the monumental building behind us that was dedicated to human justice—to the law—that attempt, anyway, at justice.

When E. left, when she rounded the corner on her bike, I called my lawyer friend. "Come on, Andrea, it's over," he said. The divorce was only a formality. "Yeah, right" was all I said, and hung up. It was clearly not over, clearly an unfinished act, a love story that, in spite of the legal steps, would keep trying to end every day, colliding every day with that official ruling. It had only been cropped, an intermediate ending, a failed, unfinished ending.

I stopped being a professional writer, as I'd promised myself, at the end of my Bavarian retreat. I took on two jobs to make a living. I stopped giving readings; I turned down every invitation to get on a stage, to provide thoughts like little beach snacks, to receive applause, have my picture taken, pretend to know how to live or at least how to think. In the meantime, three years ago, my son was born, and I married for the second time.

Every day, for months, while my son slept, between the hours of 4:00 and 7:00 a.m., I wrote another novel. So I fell once again into writing, and will probably keep falling. I stopped being a professional writer, but I haven't stopped writing. I surrender to the trap of words because silence is overwhelming, and crushes my temples. So I have to break it with a sentence, shatter it, carry some words to safety, outside myself. Every time I do this, I think it's the last time, and while I'm doing it, I also feel like doing it is a failure. But perhaps it's worth it to reach this limit, to fail this way, to write only when not writing would be dying, to write only when I can't do otherwise.

During his final days, in the Kierling sanatorium, Kafka couldn't speak: his tuberculosis of the larynx had grown worse, was choking him. So he wrote small notes and passed them to Dora Diamant or his friend Robert Klopstock. "Often offer the nurse wine," "Max has his birthday on May 27," "One must take care that the lowest flowers over there, where they have been crushed into the vases, don't suffer." Kafka's extreme writing: notes passed to a woman and to a friend, when he was dying. Isn't this Kafka's ultimate exit from literature, his surrender to life? Kafka shook off literature the way a dog shakes himself after the rain. The naked words of life remain when faced with death. When faced with silence.

Our pediatrician says I talk too much to my son, that I have to give him some space. That at age three, he just doesn't need all that stimulation. "Have you ever tried to be quiet?" he laughed over the phone, after our families had just had dinner together. "Why don't you try?" And so I've tried: I practice not talking when I'm with my son. While we play, I hold back the avalanche of words I'm tempted to drop on his head. "Don't worry—he knows you exist," the doctor told me.

That silence—or at least trying to be silent—is all I have learned, that jump into the void, which writing can't do. That silence—I'd like never to break it; I'd like to feel that I didn't have to roll it up, like coiled rope, to make a story of it, a thought, a request for help. I'd like not to write anymore.

I sometimes watch my son playing by himself. I keep my distance, in the doorway to his room. Now and then I'll call my wife to come and see. We stay there awhile, watching. Then she goes back to what she was doing, and I stay where I am. There's a piercing intensity to the sight of your son learning to play by himself. An absolute loneliness, which he knows how to inhabit. And a different loneliness, yours, in the doorway to his room, which is harder to maintain. Every time, I feel the urge to walk in, to say, *Amore mio*, and save him, and save myself, with those two words. But I don't—I hold back, try to keep these words to myself. My unfinished words. It takes more strength, more courage, to hold them back than to go into his room and finish the story by saying, *Amore mio*. So I keep quiet.

But then I go in and say, "Amore mio." And once again I fail, and once again I'm human. ✶

AN INCOMPLETE LIST OF UNFINISHED WORKS

A PARTIAL HISTORY OF THE HALF-DONE,
THE DELAYED, THE DISCARDED, THE SHELVED,
THE ABANDONED, AND THE SCRAPPED

*compiled by Emily Lang, Molly Main,
Sunra Thompson, and Katherine Williams*

The Canterbury Tales *by Geoffrey Chaucer*

Started: 1387; **Stopped:** 1400

The Faerie Queene *by Edmund Spenser*

Started: 1589; **Stopped:** 1596

The Art of Fugue *by Johann Sebastian Bach*

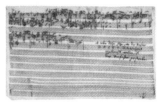

Started: 1740; **Stopped:** 1746

Maria: or, The Wrongs of Woman *by Mary Wollstonecraft*

Started: 1797; **Stopped:** 1797

Salvator Mundi *by Albrecht Dürer*

Started: 1505; **Stopped:** 1505

Unfinished Portrait of General Bonaparte *by Jacques-Louis David*

Started: 1797; **Stopped:** 1798

Siena Cathedral
by Giovanni di Agostino, Camaino di Crescentino, and Giovanni Pisano

Started: 1215; **Stopped:** 1263

The Entombment *by Michelangelo*

Started: 1500; **Stopped:** 1501

The Athenaeum Portrait *by Gilbert Stuart*

Started: 1796; **Stopped:** 1796

Madame X *by Auguste Rodin*

Started: 1907; **Stopped:** 1907

Take Your Son, Sir!
by Ford Madox Brown

Started: 1851; **Stopped:** 1856

National Monument of Scotland
by Charles Robert Cockerell and William Henry Playfair

Started: 1823; **Stopped:** 1829

La Sagrada Família

Started: 1852; **Stopped:** 1926

American Commissioners of the Preliminary Peace Agreement with Great Britain (Treaty of Paris)
by Benjamin West

Started: 1783; Stopped: 1783

New York City, 3 *by Piet Mondrian*

Started: 1941; Stopped: 1941

Sathorn Unique Tower
by Rangsan Torsuwan

Started: 1990; Stopped: 1997

THE
UNFINISHED NOVELS OF FRANZ KAFKA

Amerika
Started: 1911; Stopped: 1914

....

The Trial
Started: 1914; Stopped: 1915

....

The Castle
Started: 1922; Stopped: 1922

The Cathedral of St. John the Divine *by Heins & LaFarge*

Started: 1892; Stopped: 1941

RMMV *Oceanic* *by Harland & Wolff*

Started: 1926; Stopped: 1928

Crazy Horse Memorial *by Korczak Ziolkowski*

Started: 1948; **Stopped:** —

Dune *by Alejandro Jodorowsky*

Started: 1974; **Stopped:** 1976

Foreshore Freeway Bridge *by Solomon "Solly" Simon Morris*

Started: 1970s; **Stopped:** 1977

Versailles (Florida)

Started: 2004; **Stopped:** —

The Cincinnati Subway *by Henry Thomas Hunt*

Started: 1920; **Stopped:** 1927

Even as their cities are bombed, Ukrainians continue to fill their malls with electronics, host classical music concerts, and import tropical fruits—acts of resistance in the face of Russia's attempts to destroy the fabric of their society.

SKETCHES FROM UKRAINE

by **DAVE EGGERS**   *illustrations by* **TETIANA YAKUNOVA**

The stores were all full. We noticed it in our first minutes in Ukraine. We'd crossed the border from Poland in early December, and after passing through the Polish checkpoint, then the Ukrainian checkpoint, we stopped at a gas station that had a café within, and we were surprised to find that it was immaculate and well stocked. There were three women in uniforms working at the small lunch counter. A trucker sat at a blond-wood table, eating a fresh crepe.

Anything that you could find or want was there. There was coffee from Ethiopia. There were chips and soda and high-quality chocolates. There was fresh fruit. There was liquor of any kind. There were books. There were mugs that celebrated the Ukrainian military.

I bought two such mugs. One bore the Ukrainian logo, and the other had a graphic of a hand throwing a Molotov cocktail accompanied by the words UKRAINIAN SMOOTHIE. When we got back to the van, our driver, a middle-aged Ukrainian, saw my mugs and insisted on helping me wrap them to make sure they wouldn't be damaged in my backpack. First he used tissue paper. Then, finding that insufficient, he went to the gas pumps, and found that cloth used to clean oil dipsticks, and returned, insisting on wrapping my mugs himself. He did not want those mugs, with their defiant messages, to come to harm.

I was not expecting that there would be clean and well-stocked gas stations all over Ukraine. I did not expect every store in Lviv and Kyiv to be full and well lit and spotless. I did not expect to be able to buy Christmas ornaments made to look like Ukrainian soldiers in masks and carrying Sidewinder RPGs.

I bought one of these, and bought toilet paper bearing the face of Vladimir Putin. All over Kyiv we ate at sophisticated cafés and restaurants—Crimean food, Georgian food, haute Ukrainian cuisine made by a celebrity chef named Ievgen Klopotenko, who had trained at Le Cordon Bleu and now wanted to prove to the world that borscht

was not a Russian invention but was Ukrainian, one of so many things and people (Gogol, Bulgakov) that were Ukrainian but had been co-opted by the Russians, then the Soviets, then the Russians. It had to stop.

I believe that in the West we have not gotten a full picture of life in Ukraine during war. It is infinitely richer and more alive and inspiring than we are led to believe. The city of Kyiv in the first week of December was frantic with cars, with commuters, with Christmas music, with candlelight concerts, with shoppers. The stores were open. The nail salons were open. The movie theaters were open. The tattoo parlors were open. The bars were open. One night we sat in an underground pub, drinking local stout, when a large man in a Ukrainian military uniform walked in with his girlfriend, who wore a cat-eared tiara. They sat at a lacquered table, talking with bright eyes, holding hands, until another man came in, with a dog on a leash. The man seemed to be the soldier's brother or friend and they hadn't seen each other in a while. The two men embraced, while the dog, a muscular black mutt, whined and spun with vaulting joy. The soldier leaned down to pet and wrestle the dog, and finally everyone sat again, the mutt under the table, draped over the soldier's feet, soon asleep. The World Cup was on TV.

I went to Ukraine as part of a PEN America delegation bringing attention to Russia's attempts at erasing the history and culture of Ukraine. Because this is a key element of the Russian strategy—to absorb Ukraine, they must convince the world, and some percentage of Ukrainians, that Ukraine never really was a separate nation, a distinct people. The delegation was led by PEN's director, Suzanne Nossel, and included the writers Peter Godwin and Barbara Demick, and members of PEN's staff in the United States and Ukraine. We toured sites of Russian war crimes around Kyiv, met with local leaders, and students and writers, activists and passersby, and we were crushed by the useless waste of life that Putin made possible, and at the same time moved by the undentable resolve of every last Ukrainian we met. Contrary to Russian military theory, every new attack, every fresh atrocity, only makes Ukraine stronger.

I want to tell you about the wretched suffering that you have seen and read about, but if you will permit me, I'd also like to tell you that Ukraine is an almost fully functioning nation that defies one's expectations for the conditions of life during wartime. This is not to say that the war raging in the eastern part of the country was not being felt in the capital. It was. It was on everyone's minds at all times. The once-weekly air strikes were on everyone's minds. The power outages were talked about, workarounds were settled upon. The chief guide at the National Museum of the History of Ukraine told us that when the electricity goes out, and she can't take the

train in to work, she walks six kilometers through the snow and slush to get to the museum, which is empty. In the days after Russia invaded Ukraine, they emptied the museum of most of its eight hundred thousand objects. We visited the museum, and were interrupted by an air raid, during which over seventy

missiles were sent to Ukraine from Belarus. More on that later. We met a philosophy professor who once a month buys and drives used cars to soldiers who need them to get to the front. We met a young couple who fosters dogs abandoned during the fighting. We met a groundskeeper at an elementary school who gave us a tour—will give

anyone a tour—of the basement where he, his family, and three hundred and fifty others from their town were held hostage by Russian soldiers for twenty-eight days, and where twelve people died. We saw the mass grave behind St. Andrew's Church in Bucha, where Ukrainians had to bury their own—one hundred and sixteen civilians killed in the first days of the invasion. We saw the Banksy on a crumbling, fire-licked building in Borodyanka. In a library in Chernihiv, we saw the hole where a Russian missile had torn through the roof, but on the first floor we saw a group of women who were taking Ukrainian lessons. Until then they'd spoken only Russian.

Everywhere we went we saw a rebirth of Ukrainian identity. In 2014 and in the buildup to this invasion, the Russians had sought to diminish the distinctiveness of Ukrainian culture and identity, claiming that the country had always been part of Russia, and would be again—that 40 percent of the country already spoke Russian as their first language. They sought to water down, to swallow Ukrainian identity, to absorb it into Russia as they had again and again before. But Putin's invasion has produced the opposite effect: Every Ukrainian we met was aglow with national pride, and to the last person we spoke to, they loathed all of Russia with molten fury. The librarians and literature students would no longer read Dostoyevsky or Pushkin—both of whom were considered propagandists for Russian imperialism. We went to a classical music showcase one snowy night, packed with well-dressed couples and families and a few soldiers, too, and though the musicians played Mendelssohn and Mozart and Bach, Tchaikovsky was notably absent. Anything Russian had been banished. The Russians past and present were orcs, animals, complicit, and soon would be defeated. Everyone expected victory over the Russians—we never heard the least bit of doubt, ever, from anyone—but what would happen afterward was considered the hard part. How to relate to their aggressors, and to a nation of silent Russians who enabled the invasion, after the war?

"I just can't imagine it," said Anna Shcherbiak, a PhD student. She and her boyfriend, Andrii Fedotov, had brought us to a bustling restaurant called Musafir, opened by Crimean refugees who fled the fighting in 2014.

"In 2014," Anna said, "there were Russian liberals opposed to the war. Now there are no Russians you can connect with. Why don't these people feel guilt? I want them to recognize this. I want them to say, *I'm guilty.*"

It is not hard to get into Ukraine. Fly to Kraków or Warsaw and get on the road. Or take a train. The border takes a while—about two hours—then you're in. There are thousands of vehicles, and dozens of trains, going in and out of the country every day. The drive from Kraków to Lviv takes four hours. Kyiv is another seven. The hotel where we stayed in Kyiv, the Radisson Blu, had power continuously and was filled with Americans and Europeans. There were evangelicals from Tennessee and Alabama, there were Catholic priests from England and Scotland, there were German mercenaries, there was a gathering of the Danish Refugee Council. Each morning, some mix of all these groups would populate the dining room for the breakfast buffet, which was just short of extravagant. There were vats of sausages and bacon. There were pancakes and waffles and seasoned potatoes cut into small wedges. There were eggs any way you'd like. There were croissants, pastries, a half dozen kinds of cereal. There were a dozen cheeses and yogurts. There were oranges, bananas, persimmons, pineapples, cucumbers, and peppers. All in Ukraine in December.

This is not to diminish the deprivation felt at the front. This is only to demonstrate Ukrainian resilience. Russian aggression will not prevent them from having their pineapples in December. It will not prevent them from filling their malls with new electronics. One day in Bucha, which was hit hard in the war's early days, we visited a mall that had every new television, every new phone, and was brightly lit and full of shoppers. Next door was the ruin of an outdoor market that Russian rockets had reduced to twisted metal. That and so many ruins had the look of World War II—the snow-covered rubble, the fire-stained concrete skeletons of homes and factories and markets. But then so often, next door, there were brand-new malls with their twenty-first-century goods, there were karaoke bars and pole-dancing exercise studios. There was Uber. A stone's throw from neighborhoods flattened by Russian bombs, developers were building new condominiums.

North of Kyiv, construction cranes were everywhere. If Ukraine is not the most resilient and defiant nation currently on Earth, please show me what is.

They are getting on with things.

The soldiers take trains east, or drive used cars to the front, and the rest of the population gets on with things. School must be taught. Trucks must transport goods. Cars parked in the wrong spot must be towed.

One afternoon we watched a tow truck appear in front of our hotel and, in less than three minutes, remove a car that was parked too close to an alleyway. It was the thousandth example of everyday life going on as before, and I found it so startling that I filmed it. The two men in the tow truck saw me filming, and they seemed to recognize how odd the whole thing seemed—towing away a car in the middle of a war—so when they finished, in under three minutes—it really was extraordinary—they waved to me and gave a thumbs-up as they sped off.

The two men in the tow truck looked to be in their early thirties, and seeing young men towing a car, and not fighting Russians, was something we had gotten used to. The streets of Lviv and Kyiv are full of young men and women of fighting age who are not fighting. There are healthy young people making coffee at restaurants. There are healthy young men and women studying at the university and working at McDonald's. There are young men standing guard at high-end apartment buildings and gift shops. When the war began, Ukraine instituted a ban on any men between ages eighteen and sixty leaving the country until the war was over, and everyone in our delegation assumed this meant the cities would be largely devoid of men in this age range. But they were everywhere.

Early in our visit, I'd tried, as delicately as possible, to ask some of the young men we met how they had managed to avoid military service thus far. The answers varied. One tall, athletic man said he had not passed the physical. Another said he thought he was signed up for the draft, but hadn't heard

But there is not yet a full mobilization. There is not yet the kind of draft that sends all young men to war. So there are thousands of young people all over the streets of the cities and suburbs, going about their business—working, studying, bartending. We went to the Kyiv Zoo one day—it's open! In the dead of winter!—and though its inhabitants live a profoundly sad existence, next to the zoo is a university,

his restaurant, called Rokiv 100, a three-story establishment, Scandinavian in design, warm and clean, and full to the brim with stylish diners on a Tuesday night in December. As we sat down, one of our Ukrainian hosts told us that the chef was very well known and well regarded. He'd been trained at Le Cordon Bleu, he'd written books, was often on TV, had fed refugees in Lviv when the war was new. We ate fish

anything from his government. It was hard to untangle the rules of who had to serve and when, but here is a very simplified version: There is a standing army of professional soldiers, just as most countries maintain. A huge portion of these soldiers were trained by American advisers after the 2014 invasion—partly in anticipation of another invasion. In addition, there are those who signed up early in the war and by now are well-trained and seasoned soldiers. Then there are new volunteers.

and classes were in full swing, with hundreds of laughing young students trundling by on the icy sidewalks. That there could be hundreds of thousands of young men and women who are able to fight but are not fighting during this existential war is one of the many complexities that many generally informed people might not know.

I also did not know about the star restaurateur named Ievgen Klopotenko, the one I mentioned earlier. Our group had dinner one night at

soup and potato mousse and galyshki, all of it excellent, the menu a mix of traditional and playful—even including a dish called "fried honey bees." Late in the evening, we ordered the bees, and they arrived in a little black heap of bodies and wings, with a length of honeycomb making a sort of roof over the pile of dead insects. Some in our party ate the bees, which had no notable taste, and the rest of us had more sparkling wine from Odesa, and then the chef himself appeared.

He was young, thirty-five, with a tangle of curly reddish hair, shaved tight on the sides. He wore a yellow sweater and capri pants and bright red sneakers. When he appeared from the kitchen, the patrons of the restaurant all looked up, briefly awed. Then he held court at our table, telling us the many ways in which Russians had tried to appropriate Ukrainian cuisine. Borscht is a Ukrainian dish, he said, and the Russians had claimed it. For years Klopotenko had been trying to convince the world that borscht was Ukrainian; he'd even submitted an application to UNESCO to have it so recognized. More than simply claiming many Ukrainian dishes, the Russians, he said, had waged a centuries-long war on spices. In particular, oregano.

He pronounced it "or-eh-GHAN-o," and spoke for ten minutes, in skilled but tumbling English, about the Russians' war on oregano. It was highly entertaining, and very unexpected, to be hearing about a war on an Italian spice in the middle of this grim Ukrainian winter.

Next to me was the writer and philosopher Volodymyr Yermolenko, who in a few days' time was heading toward the front, driving a used Mitsubishi he had bought for a Ukrainian soldier—a former student of his. She'd been studying literature last year, at the Taras Shevchenko National University of Kyiv. Then she joined the army, and needed a way to get to the fighting.

"You can come if you'd like," he said.

I didn't understand why he was bringing a car to a soldier. Weren't there troop transport vehicles?

"No, no," he explained. In this war, Ukrainian soldiers are not brought to the front via military trucks or

planes. No, for the most part, they drive themselves to the front. And in many cases, they need vehicles. So people like Volodymyr, too old to fight, have been donating used cars to these soldiers, so the soldiers can then drive them to Bakhmut and the Donbas. At the front, these cars are usually abandoned.

The drive to Kherson would take Volodymyr about ten hours. A friend of his would be following him, and would drive him back. They did this trip once a month. They'd donated eight cars already.

I wanted to go. I took his number. We all left Klopotenko's restaurant and met the cold, snowy Kyiv night. Some of the buildings were dark. Some were brightly lit. In the city center, it was hard to figure out who had electricity, when, and why. Every hotel and major restaurant seemed unaffected by the blackouts. Meanwhile, all the civilians we met dealt with long blackouts— four hours, eight hours. Often they answered emails late, apologizing, citing that they'd been without power since the day before. Not that anyone complained. No one complained. There were always people, millions, who had it worse. We parted ways with everyone who'd come to dinner— students and writers, activists and philosophers.

The next day, many of them were going to Kharkiv, an all-day drive, to attend the funeral of Volodymyr Vakulenko, a politically active writer of prose and books for children, who had joined the Ukrainian struggle, and had been kidnapped from his home and was missing for months. Finally, when the Russians retreated from Kharkiv, his body was found. Until it was identified by his family, it was known as Body 319. He'd been shot twice and left in the street.

The next afternoon, Peter Godwin and I were back in that neighborhood. A few blocks from Klopotenko's restaurant is the National Museum of the History of Ukraine, a stately gray building, Roman in design, and now surrounded by sandbags. To get warm—it was ten degrees and felt colder than that—we went in. The lobby had been transformed into an exhibit of recent artifacts of the Russian invasion—street signs riddled with bullet holes, a child's pillow pierced by a bullet. In the light-filled stairway just off the main floor, pieces of shrapnel and Russian bombs had been hung from the ceiling, making a grim installation of rusted steel.

A guide approached. Her name was Svitlana. She wore skinny jeans and an orange faux-fur vest. We asked her if we could see the rest of the museum. She told us that much of the museum was empty, that the most precious of its eight hundred thousand artifacts were hidden, to avoid being looted by Russian forces. We asked if we could see the museum anyway. She called the museum's press secretary, and, after a few minutes of intense conversation, she got permission to give us a tour.

"But the cashier isn't here yet," Svitlana said. She asked us to wait, so we sat down on a bench in the lobby, next to a couple of Ukrainian women who looked to be in their seventies. They were bundled up in heavy down coats and rubber boots.

Soon Svitlana approached again.

"I'm sorry," she said. "There is an air raid. We must go downstairs."

These days in Kyiv, news of air raids is more commonly communicated by smartphones than by sirens. We followed her to the basement.

Downstairs, a group of older docents were huddled together in a

carpeted room used for children's education. We sat with Svitlana in the adjoining hallway, brightly lit and covered in gray tile. The hallway was unheated, so we kept our coats on. We asked how long the air raids usually lasted.

"Sometimes an hour, sometimes two," she said.

Her full name was Svitlana Slastennikova. She was in her thirties, with blond hair, a heart-shaped face, and an earnest disposition. Her fingernails were painted red and matched her phone case. Hunched forward on a bench, she opened an app that allowed her to track Russian missiles in the air.

She clicked her tongue. "Oh, it's bad," she said.

The technology is now so advanced that Ukrainian citizens can know, more or less in real time, where the Russian missiles are coming from and generally where they're going. In this case, Russia had just launched some seventy missiles, headed to sites all over Ukraine. The assumption was that they were directed at power substations, meant to cripple the country's electrical grid. Vladimir Putin's recent strategy has been to knock out the power in the depth of winter in hopes of breaking the spirits of everyday Ukrainians.

So far this strategy has not worked.

"My friends and I, we have jokes about it," she said. "At home I organize all my housework during the hours I have power." She and her husband, a doctor who runs a private medical clinic, recently bought an inverter, which stores power when the grid is functioning. "I'm ready to be without electricity, but not a part of the Russian world, you know?"

Svitlana was born in 1986, "the year of Chernobyl," she said. She's worked at the museum for thirteen years, but her work has grown more urgent since 2014. When the Russians invaded the Donbas and annexed Crimea, Ukrainians wanted to learn more about their history as a people, independent of Russia. Because she finds so many Ukrainians, and foreign visitors, confused about the distinct histories of Ukraine and Russia, Svitlana wrote, and is now translating into English, a lecture titled "Ukrainians vs. Russians. Why Are We Not 'Fraternal' Nations?" It details the distinct history of Ukraine, going back centuries. "We're not the same people," she says. "Ethnically, we're totally different from Russians."

For years, Svitlana had been giving tours inside the museum, but immediately after the February 2022 invasion, the staff closed the building. Before the war, the museum employed about three hundred, but around 20 percent of the staff left when the war started and have not returned. Now, on any given day, between fifty and seventy curators, guides, archivists, and other staff members are on site, she says, and they have to fulfill their educational mission without many of the museum's holdings.

"At the moment," Svitlana says, "we have lectures, lectures, lectures."

Meanwhile, Putin has made every effort to erase Ukrainian identity. His troops have ransacked museums and churches, bombed schools and cultural centers, and have fed Russian-speaking Ukrainians in occupied regions a constant diet of propaganda asserting that Ukrainians are Russians, and always have been. Before the 2022 invasion, even Svitlana's own mother had believed some of the messaging coming from Moscow.

"When the Russians first invaded in February," Svitlana said, "my mother told me, 'In one month we will be part of Russia.' I said to her, 'You are insane.'"

This is part of the generational divide in Ukraine. Those who grew up in Soviet times are often more sanguine about Russian control, while those who grew up after Ukraine's independence, in 1991, often look to Europe, not Moscow, as their past and future. The fierce resistance put up by Ukrainian troops, and the atrocities committed by Russian soldiers, have shocked many older Ukrainians.

"My mother, when she saw how wild these Russians are," Svitlana said, "she changed her mind. These crimes being committed in the twenty-first century? Now she doesn't want to be part of Russia." Her mother, like millions of Ukrainians, is fluent in both Russian and Ukrainian. But many people now choose to speak Ukrainian, even if they grew up speaking Russian.

Svitlana's phone pinged again.

"Oh no. This is real," she said. Her app had more detail now. The missiles appeared to be heading toward targets all over the country: west toward Lviv, Ternopil, and Khmelnytskyi, south toward Kryvyi Rih, and north toward Kyiv.

Peter and I were getting texts now from friends in Ukraine, telling us to get somewhere safe. In recent weeks, the danger was most acute near any of the power substations. Residents could be hit either by the missile itself or, more likely, by a fragment of that missile after the Ukrainian military had shot it from the sky.

But the members of the museum staff, as we'd been talking to Svitlana

in the basement, were moving up and down the stairs, seemingly unworried about the missiles in the air. A cleaning woman had been busy with the basement's two bathrooms; she hadn't paused once since the raid began.

We heard the scuffling of footsteps on the stairs. A group of people trundled down, two adults and a teenager in a sweatshirt bearing the face of Johnny Depp. They'd been outside and had come into the museum for shelter. They went into the carpeted classroom and sat next to a whiteboard featuring a handwritten time line of Ukraine's history.

Online, we could see images of families massing in the subways of Kyiv. Built during Soviet times in anticipation of nuclear war, the subway stations are among the deepest in the world— some as far as three hundred feet below street level. I asked if Svitlana needed to check in with her own husband and kids. No, she said. She had already gotten word on her phone that they were sheltering in place. Her kids' school had a basement they used during raids.

"They started practicing before the invasion began," she said. "I didn't approve of this. I thought it was scary to the kids, to have them doing these drills." Like so many Ukrainians, Svitlana didn't think the invasion would actually happen—even when a hundred thousand Russian troops were amassing at the border.

Her son is twelve and her daughter is five, and by now they're used to the drills. Her children play games while they shelter in place. At the beginning of the invasion, Svitlana had taken her kids west for a couple of months, but now that the fighting has moved to the eastern front, she is content to stay in Kyiv. With every Ukrainian victory, more residents of the city have returned from elsewhere in Europe and the western part of the country. "I can't imagine living in Poland. Living in some gymnasium," she said. Her husband, like all men between eighteen and sixty, is barred from leaving the country anyway.

Svitlana checked her phone again.

"Explosions reported in Vinnytsia," she said. This was southwest of Kyiv. She put her phone down. She scoffed at the Russian strategy. Using Telegram, she'd been able to watch Russian political talk shows—those surreal programs where pundits expound on the war in a TV studio resembling the set of *Weakest Link*.

"They were saying they have to continue to hit these electrical targets, because they want people to rise up and overthrow the government. To get rid of Zelensky. They want it to be like Maidan," she said, referring to the 2013–14 Ukrainian movement that pushed for closer relations with the EU and resulted in the fall of the country's government. "It is insane. They do not understand us."

The teenager in the Johnny Depp sweatshirt and her parents emerged, shrugging into their coats. They made their way up the stairs and left the building. The air raid was still on, but, these days, Ukrainians are willing to sit still for only so long. Peter and I thanked Svitlana and left at about

two o'clock, an hour into the raid. The day was clear and cold, and eventually the sidewalks filled up with pedestrians. Stores and bars were open, and there was virtually no sign that Kyiv was under attack. Which it was.

Later we found out that over sixty of the more than seventy rockets had

been shot down by Ukrainian forces. The ten or so missiles that found their targets shut off electricity in at least six regions: Zhytomyr, Sumy, Zaporizhzhia, Dnipro, Cherkasy, and Kharkiv. This was the sixth large-scale attack on infrastructure since October 10, and would not be the last. Four civilians were reportedly killed,

bringing the total dead to well over sixty-five hundred, including more than four hundred children.

As evening came on, we entered the closest subway station and stepped onto the escalator. We moved at an alarming speed, through a concrete tunnel, descending into the bowels of the earth while triumphant signs greeted us left and right—children's drawings of Ukrainian soldiers. When we finally reached the train platform, we expected it to be empty, or full of families sheltering in place, but instead we saw a few dozen commuters waiting for trains, in office clothing, heading home from work.

Then, when the first train arrived, a thousand Ukrainians poured from it like water from a broken dam. They flowed around us so quickly we had to throw our backs against the station's wide concrete columns. The people of Kyiv were entirely uncowed.

We returned to the street level to find the city's lights on and bright. A café next to the train station was blasting "Santa Claus Is Coming to Town" from a tinny speaker. A nearby storefront featured, in foot-high letters, the slogan BRAVERY IS UKRAINIAN BRAND. We checked the time: we had twenty minutes to get across town. Our new Ukrainian friends, Anna and Andrii, had invited us to dinner at a celebrated Crimean Tatar restaurant, opened by refugees after the 2014 annexation. When the air raid began, we had wondered if our dinner would be canceled. But no. When we arrived, the place was full.

We joined Anna and Andrii in the last empty seats.

Peter and I had met Anna Shcherbiak a few days before. She had promised to show us this restaurant, Musafir, opened by Crimean refugees in 2015. She is twenty-seven, a PhD student with dark hair and bright eyes. With her was her boyfriend, Andrii Fedotov, a curly-haired thirty-two-year-old with liquid eyes and Invisalign braces on his teeth. As the waitress, in traditional Tatar dress, handed us menus and poured water and wine, we talked first about the air raid, and how odd it was to be eating out a few hours later.

"It *is* surreal," Anna said. "We were saying this morning, we woke up and there's no electricity, and we said, 'It's fine.' You can't let it get to you. If it does, it will break you. The life we live right now—for us to continue doing what we're doing—is already an act of defiance."

Anna went to college outside Chicago and is now getting a doctorate in business administration at the University of Vienna. Andrii just finished a master's in social entrepreneurship in Bulgaria—with all the classes taught in French. Andrii speaks French and German, in addition to English, Ukrainian, and Russian. Anna speaks Ukrainian, Russian, Mandarin, English, and Spanish. She can talk in great detail about the tonal differences between Mandarin and Cantonese—she lived in Hong Kong for a time—and with great humor about learning Spanish because she fell in love with a Colombian. Her English is almost perfect, with an endearing Midwestern tint.

They have lived all over the world, and could live anywhere now. But

they're staying in Kyiv until the war is over. Anna and Andrii exemplify a specific part of the Ukrainian population—well-educated and worldly young people who, like Svitlana, have never lived under Russian rule and will never accept it. At the same time, their family relationships with Russia are complicated. Extremely so.

Anna's family is ethnically Ukrainian, going back as many generations as Anna can track, but the men in her family often lived in Russia for work, or were stationed there as members of the military. So though their roots are in Ukraine, they have been moving between Ukraine and Russia for generations. Anna's grandmother, for example, was born in Russia, but moved to Ukraine after the 1991 independence. She still speaks Russian at home, even though her children and grandchildren speak Ukrainian. "She considers herself Russian by ethnicity," Anna said, "which, judging by our family history, is not true. But she would never move to Russia. She considers Ukraine her home.

"I know it's confusing," Anna said.

Her grandmother now lives alone in Ukraine, and consumes Russian propaganda online.

"She watches YouTube," Anna said. The algorithms lead her down rabbit holes of pro-Russian narratives. "She asks, 'Why is Ukraine resisting? Why cause all this trouble? Can't Zelensky negotiate something?'"

Her son, though—Anna's father—was born in Ukraine, and considers himself Ukrainian. As does Anna.

She and Andrii are uncompromising about the Russians who have done nothing to stop the invasion—who, through their inaction and silence, implicitly support it. She has a Russian friend who studies at MIT, who protested the war from the United States and feels that's all he can do.

"It's not enough," Anna said, shaking her head vigorously. "I'm risking my *life* to be here. I say, 'Not enough.' Don't say it's Putin, don't say it's the current system. Recognize that it's the history—that you have enjoyed the liberties of imperialism."

Much like Svitlana, Anna and Andrii are of a generation that was born into a revived Ukrainian identity. In 1997, Andrii was in the first class of elementary school students to get their primary instruction not in Russian but in Ukrainian.

His parents, raised in Odesa under Soviet rule, felt liberated when the Berlin Wall fell, and began traveling extensively. They lived for a time in India, where his father did business and where both parents became Buddhists. Andrii was raised in Odesa with Ukrainian spoken at home, Russian spoken on the streets and playgrounds, and both Ukrainian and English in school. Buddhism, meanwhile, didn't fit his worldview.

"Buddhism is about being outside the situation," he said, "and I like to be *in* the problem." With an eye toward building Ukraine's civil society, he got a master's in social entrepreneurship in Bulgaria—with all the instruction in French. His fellow students were from Canada, Benin, Senegal, Côte d'Ivoire, and Haiti. "We learned just as much from each other as from the coursework," he said.

Now Andrii works for GIZ, a German agency that has sought to help small towns throughout Ukraine evolve from the Soviet top-down model of government to more local control—thus creating a civil society resistant to colonization. When the invasion began in 2022, their work

was paused. The local mayors and officeholders they supported over the years were quickly targeted by the Russians. Some were jailed, some killed. Most fled west.

Our entrées arrived. The food of Tatar Crimea has echoes of the Mediterranean and the Balkans—kebabs, olives, eggplant, yogurt, hummus.

I ordered the Genghis Khan plate, a four-pound heap of lamb and beef and chicken—entirely too much food for one person. I asked if they could take any home, but Anna and Andrii are vegetarians. Anna is, anyway. Andrii is trying.

Maybe they have a dog? I asked.

Not at the moment, they said. But since the war began, they've fostered a series of dogs brought back from the front.

"There's a joke here," Anna said, "that you are not a journalist in Ukraine if you have not been asked to take a dog back from the front line." Soldiers find the dogs on the streets or in abandoned houses—sometimes still in cages—and they try to pair them with journalists heading back to Kyiv.

The restaurant began to empty. It was close to 9:00 p.m., and Kyiv's wartime curfew is 11:00. The staff would have to clean up, close up, and get home while the trains were still running. As we finished dinner, we talked about what will happen after the war is over— if there can ever be civil relations between the two countries.

Anna shook her head.

"I just can't imagine it. Before, when I went abroad and heard Russian being spoken, I would think, OK, we have a language in common. I don't know where you're from— maybe Kazakhstan, maybe Ukraine— but it's already a connection point. Now it's not a connection point. Now when people say, 'Do you speak Russian?,' I say no."

The atrocities are too fresh.

There is a small town two hours from Kyiv called Yahidne. Before the invasion, about four hundred people lived there. It is located just off the main highway that connects Kyiv to towns in the north, and eventually to Belarus. This convenient location made it a Russian target.

On March 3, 2022, Russian soldiers surrounded the town from all sides. They kicked down doors and brought the residents to the local school, where they were held hostage. Three hundred and fifty men, women, and children were huddled into the school's basement and were forced to stay there, without heat or electricity, for the next twenty-eight days.

I should say that this story has been told. Journalists have been to this town. On the ride to Yahidne, someone mentioned this, that the story of Yahidne has been "picked over." To some extent this is true. AP and Reuters have written stories about what happened there. Meanwhile, the victims of certain war crimes are not satisfied with a handful of accounts. They are willing to show visitors what happened, in hopes that the story will be known widely and that this might ensure that the perpetrators are held accountable. So whether or not you have heard this story before, I'd like to tell it again.

On a frozen morning, a man named Ivan Polguy met us outside the local elementary school. Before the war, he was the groundskeeper there. Ivan is a sturdy man of sixty-two, with a pink face, blue eyes, and a walrus mustache. He wore jeans, work boots, and a leather jacket with sheepskin lining. It was ten degrees outside and his breath appeared in gray gusts. His black wool hat was pulled tight to his forehead, but he wore no gloves.

The Russian invasion began on February 24, but Yahidne could not have expected to be part of the conflict. Its residents assumed that the Russian army would continue past their town, on their way to Kyiv. But on the morning of March 3, the town was rattled by artillery fire and tanks.

"The sky and earth was on fire," Ivan said. "Then the soldiers came from the woods." With his bare hand, he pointed to the woods north of the town—tall pines dusted this day in snow.

The groundskeeper's phone rang. It was a gentle, jangly tone. He turned away to answer it. A cat, black with white paws, raced past, cutting under a play structure with one rusted swing. He turned back and continued.

The people in the town tried to escape, he said, but the Russian soldiers blocked all exits. Those who tried to get on the highway to leave were shot dead. The soldiers then went from house to house, disabling cars and communication devices. "They took out batteries and slashed tires," Ivan said. "They confiscated phones and computers."

Most of the Ukrainians living in Yahidne were brought to the basement of the local elementary school. The Russians painted the words CHILDREN INSIDE on the school to thwart any attacks on their position from the Ukrainian military. The residents of the town were being used as human shields.

Over the next few days, the Russians set up artillery positions, communications stations, and commandeered most of the local houses. They slept there, and looted anything of value. Yahidne was being used as a Russian base from which to stage the attack on Chernihiv, a much larger city, and a stepping stone to Kyiv.

I asked how many Russians were in the town.

"I can't even imagine the number," he said.

He brought us to the back of the school. There was a large square trench in the yard. The Russians had dug it, and soldiers had been stationed there to prevent anyone from leaving the school. Now it was filled with garbage and covered in snow.

"There were snipers on the roof too," Ivan said, pointing to the top of the school building, a long three-story structure of white brick. Most of the windows were boarded up. He led us into the basement.

The stairway was dark and crowded with tires and old clothes spilling from bent cardboard boxes. We descended to a tight hallway, which connected the basement's four rooms. Three rooms, usually used for storage, were no more than concrete caves.

"The whole basement is one hundred and ninety-five meters," he said. "That meant one half meter per person." There were about fifty children among the hostages.

There was no electricity in the basement, then or now. Our flashlights illuminated the dank chambers. Coat hangers gripped the water pipes attached to the ceiling. During the occupation, cloth had been hung from the wire to create some separation between the rooms and hallway. Those who were able to stay in the smaller rooms were considered lucky; they had slightly more space and less risk of disease.

The last room was more finished, about the size of a classroom, with linoleum floors and plastered walls. The largest group of hostages were kept here—one hundred and thirty-six adults and thirty-nine children. Ivan was with his wife and two children. He showed us four small metal chairs facing each other, two by two. No one could move. It was too crowded. Most of the adults could not lie down—there was not enough space. "We slept standing up," he said.

We shone our flashlights around the room, catching ghostly objects in gray light. Tiny chairs and tables were strewn about. There were a few children's beds painted purple and green. The ground was covered in coloring books, wrappers, shreds of clothing, and rubble.

Before the Russians sequestered them in the basement, the hostages grabbed what they could from home and from the school's cafeteria. They had to ration and share this food for the next month.

"Sometimes the Russians would give the kids some candy or waffles and then take a picture," he said—propaganda to imply the hostages were being treated well.

The younger soldiers stayed on the first floor of the school, and were often

drunk. "They would come down and tell the kids they could play with their guns. They gave them grenades and told them they could hold them, as long as they didn't pull the pin."

The basement was airless and the hostages were not allowed to leave to relieve themselves. Ivan pointed to a small closet-sized space off the main room. "We put the bucket there," he said.

Once every few days, a hostage would be allowed to bring the bucket of waste up the stairs and dump it in the forest.

But the Russians did not communicate well, and the hostages dumping the bucket were often shot at by other Russian soldiers, who took them for enemy soldiers. They retreated quickly back to the basement, where the smell of so many humans and human waste in proximity was wretched. Diseases were rampant.

"Everyone was sick," he said.

The older hostages began dying. "They could have lived many years more," he said. "Down here, they went crazy first."

When someone died, the residents covered the body as best they could, trying to keep the corpses away from the children. Occasionally the hostages were given permission to bring the bodies to the forest for burial. Men would carry each body up the stairs and put it in a wheelbarrow. They would stack two or three bodies and then wheel the bodies into the trees, where they would dig shallow graves in the frozen ground.

Again, Russian soldiers would shoot at them if they had not been alerted that a burial had been approved.

Ivan showed us a calendar handwritten on the plaster wall. Each day that someone died, their names were recorded. Twelve in all died in the basement. Next to the calendar, children had drawn flowers, hearts, a Martian.

"The soldiers kept saying they would move us soon," he said. "Always the next day, then the next day."

Ironically, it was the Russians' lack of success taking Kyiv that delayed the hostages' release. The longer it took for the Russians to advance south, the longer the town was used as a staging ground.

"The soldiers would show us propaganda that said they were winning," he said. "They said that Zelensky had capitulated, that they had taken Kyiv."

Finally, the hostages heard the earth rattle above. Then it was quiet again. They ventured from the basement and found that the Russians had left.

We followed Ivan up the stairs and into the frozen yard. His eyes were red

homes and kept three hundred and fifty people hostage, were Tuvinians.

How did he know? we asked.

"They spoke Tuvinian!" he said, and there was a burst of laughter all around. We needed that release.

Then, as we stood outside in the frozen afternoon, the horror became

powers—Turkey, then China, and finally Russia. The first major investment Russia made in Tuva, in the 1960s and 1970s, was in building a series of asbestos plants in the country.

In the 1990s, Tuva tried to secede from Russia, and since then has maintained a tense semiautonomous

and wet. We talked about accountability. He was optimistic that the perpetrators, at least some of them, will be named and found.

For the first time, he mentioned that the soldiers who came to Yahidne, who killed civilians and occupied their

clear. The Tuvinians are an ethnic minority of about two hundred thousand people from an area bordering Mongolia. Their history and appearance are closely linked to Mongolia, but for a thousand years Tuva has been subsumed by a succession of larger

relationship with Moscow, one complicated by the fact that Sergei Shoigu, the Russian defense minister, is a Tuvinian. In fact, entering the military is seen as one of the best ways up and out of poverty for the people of Tuva, where the average annual income is about seven thousand dollars—among the lowest of all Russian oblasts. The Tuvinians are considered hardy fighters, and are often sent on riskier missions where Russians from Moscow or Saint Petersburg would not be sent.

So they were sent to Yahidne.

Most were young. They had no doubt been told the conquering of Ukraine would be a matter of days. So they sequestered Yahidne's population in a school basement, and they looted the town. When the invasion stalled in Chernihiv, the Tuvinian soldiers stationed at Yahidne were in a quandary. They needed the civilians to serve as human shields, and they were most logically kept in one place—in the school. But they were not equipped to feed and care for three hundred and fifty civilian hostages, especially for a far longer period than expected.

Every death in Yahidne is the fault of one man, and that is Vladimir Putin. He put the Tuvinian troops in Ukraine. He pitted the people of one current Russian colony, Tuva, against those of a former Russian colony, Ukraine. In the fog of war, innocent people were killed by ignorant young men, and died due to the neglect of young men. And eventually these young men will be prosecuted for their cruelties and oversights, in a war they did not plan. They carried out the invasion, likely thinking that their unit's success in Ukraine might mean, for them, medals, promotions, job security. They could return to Tuva as heroes.

But they accomplished nothing.

By late March, they and all the Russian invaders had been expelled from the regions around Kyiv, and it was up to the locals to clean up and count the dead.

Mykhailyna Skoryk-Shkarivska, the deputy mayor of Bucha, has been counting.

"To talk about war crimes," she said, "you at least need to know the correct names and dates and reasons of death. Then you can investigate."

Mykhailyna is an efficient, straightforward woman in her early forties. She has agreed to give us a tour of the sites of Russian atrocities in Bucha, a city about twenty miles northwest of Kyiv, with a pre-war population of fifty-three thousand. She has short straw-colored hair, and on this wickedly cold December day, she wore a black Calvin Klein parka, sky blue jeans, and white sneakers. Sometimes she rode with us in a van. Sometimes she followed in her frost-covered compact car.

In the attempted invasion of Kyiv, she said, thirteen hundred civilians were killed, with four hundred and sixty of the victims in Bucha. When Russian progress was stalled in the area, the small city bore a disproportionate burden of the misery.

"They left the dead on the streets," she said. "We had heard of this kind of thing in Chechnya, but it surprised us to see it here." It's important to understand how the Ukrainians, especially older Ukrainians, expected the invasion to unfold. They did not expect atrocities. They did not expect the murder of civilians. Mykhailyna explains this dispassionately. She explains everything directly, precisely, and with no trace of emotion.

"You know, the connections between Ukrainian and Russian peoples was still strong," she said. She mentions the countless Ukrainians who have family in Russia, who worked or lived in Russia. "But after the Bucha tragedy, everything changed. We are not brothers or sisters anymore."

Four hundred and nineteen of the civilian victims were shot, tortured, or beaten to death. Thirty-nine died of natural causes, but even that classification is fluid. One victim, a thirty-four-year-old mother of three, died of a heart attack while hiding underground during a bombardment. Another woman, this one elderly, died of cardiac arrest when she saw her sister shot by Russian soldiers.

Mykhailyna's training is in information technology, not forensic science. But the job of identifying the dead has fallen to her.

"We have very difficult time identifying the people who were killed and burned," she said. "They say 'unknown person.' We don't know male, female. We know from the witness that this family was killed, but we need technology to prove this. It's one thing to know it from the people, and another thing to come before the international court and God and prove that."

Mykhailyna is from Dnipro, in Eastern Ukraine, but married and moved to Bucha with her husband, Serhii Shkarivskyi. In 2014, he was called up to fight when Russia invaded the Donbas. He was killed on August 19, 2014, by a sniper. Now she is raising their seven-year-old son, Hlib, on her own.

She ran for local office a few times before being elected to the Bucha City Council in 2022. When the invasion began, she and most local elected officials fled to Kyiv and farther west. On March 3, she brought her son to Transcarpathia, then Germany.

Local leaders who stayed were often killed.

"The mayor of Hostomel was killed," she said, "and his two assistants."

The mayor of Bucha, Anatoliy Fedoruk, was luckier.

"They showed up at his house and he said he was not the mayor, just the person who is looking after the house," Mykhailyna said. "They let him go. But they have lists of people they were looking for, and his name was on the list. And lots of deputies and active people from the region were blacklisted by the Russians. They were going from house to house and checking for those people. They would take the clothes off the men and check if there was a tattoo of a gun."

A tattoo of a gun might indicate that man was part of the military, or had been—and thus a threat to the occupying forces.

"They could execute a person just because of the tattoo. They were very well trained to control occupied territories."

Mykhailyna knew she was on a blacklist, so she fled. She returned in April, after Bucha was liberated by Ukrainian troops. Every month since then, more people return and more businesses open. During the invasion, a green corridor was created, through which civilians could flee. The Bucha region's population had been about seventy-five thousand, with fifty-three

thousand in Bucha City. All but thirty-seven hundred left during the fighting. Most of the people who had stayed are elderly, and most of the people who have returned are without children. Her son's school is still about 40 percent online, with students logging in from all over Europe, where they live in exile.

"It is easier to raise children in Europe," she said. "We need to repopulate the area, but it is hard here with the rocket attacks."

It's difficult, too, to attract and keep teachers.

"Some IT, foreign language, some history teachers have not come back," she said. "The biggest problem is the

teachers of music. They find good jobs in Germany, in Poland, in France. They're paid more, they're putting on concerts in Europe, so they don't need to come back."

The flip side, though, is that while some local culture has evaporated, global cultural figures have arrived.

"Before, we have to pay very big money to have top stars come to Bucha," she said. "Now they are coming on their own, giving free concerts. We have double situation. Less local artists, and that's bad, but we also have attention from first-level artists from all over the world."

Bono had been there in May.

"He was playing the harmonica in our church," she said.

She brought us to a powder-blue building with white trim. Set off a busy street, the building resembled a country church, with white columns and expansive windows. The building's facade was intact, but the rest was cratered. On one of the remaining external walls, sunflowers had been painted, against a sky dotted with oval white clouds.

"This was a Soviet-style cultural house," Mykhailyna said. "It was very popular in the Soviet Union to have, like, cultural houses in industrial parts of the city. It was very nice, very good concert hall, very popular among the local people."

She tried the doors to the hall. There were a few dozen bullet holes in the glass, and the white plaster columns to the left and right were splattered with mortar fire. The doors didn't give.

"Locked," she said, perplexed. Another local official who was with us checked her phone. The hall had been closed the day before—it was no longer safe to walk around inside. Outside the building, a banner had been erected that said IRPINHELP.COM with a QR code.

"This was a battlefield," she said.

There had been fighting all along this street. The bus stop in front of the concert hall had been pelted with a hundred bullets. That was ten months ago. The restoration work was slow going, and was not the first priority for local governments trying to keep the lights on. The most practical and profit-making entities—stores, restaurants, even fitness studios—have been the first to return to operation. Mykhailyna mentioned a traditional borscht restaurant that reopened recently. "It was a miracle. I will take you there later."

These businesses will, eventually, provide a tax base that will allow cultural institutions to be rebuilt. In the meantime, local governments are hoping that foreign sponsors take up restoration projects like this concert hall. Thus the QR code.

Across the street, a massive Volvo construction vehicle was knocking down the remains of a shelled apartment building. The sound was deafening. Traffic moved swiftly by. It's crucial to note that at all times, everywhere away from the front, Ukrainians were moving about more or less as they normally would. Cars sped past this shelled concert hall and destroyed apartment building

as they would have any other construction site.

We stood outside, in the parking lot, stamping our feet to try to stay warm.

"Two days ago, when it was hard," Mykhailyna said, "we put on generator, and I was trying to work, and my son was online, trying to find what to do if a nuclear bomb will come. He is seven years old. And you can't prevent them from these stories. They hear it from everywhere. And they are all ready to fight the Russians. He had handmade a weapon, and said to me, 'I will protect you.'"

The Ukrainians will not lose this war. Not in the sense that they will be subsumed by Russia, or that the Russians will get near Kyiv again. The only question is when it will end, and how it will end. If the Ukrainians were willing to give up the Donbas and Crimea, it would be over very soon. But there is no chance of Ukraine giving up either. The topic came up in about fifty conversations I had while in Ukraine, and I never heard any doubt from any person on the matter. There would be no compromise, no peace, until the 1991 borders were restored.

One day, our delegation visited the US embassy in Kyiv. Mark Stroh, the Acting Deputy Chief of Mission, met us in a large conference room surrounded by windows. With short black hair and glasses, wearing a suit and tie and unscuffed shoes, he was polite, efficient, and attentive; he nodded and took notes. He called himself a "post-conflict guy," having done stints in Afghanistan and

Syria. He apologized to the Ukrainians who were with us that he had not yet learned to speak their language.

He and the rest of the embassy staff members had left the country on February 13—eleven days before the invasion. As has been well documented, American intelligence was certain that Russia would invade, while Zelensky all but dismissed the possibility—even while one hundred thousand troops amassed at the Belarusian border. Stroh returned to Ukraine after the Russians were driven back from Kyiv. He has not been surprised by the Ukrainian resistance, nor was he surprised by Russia underestimating that resistance.

"Autocracies learn slowly," he said.

Much of Russia's intelligence about Ukraine was from the Soviet era, he said, including many of its targets. A watch manufacturing plant had recently been destroyed because the Russians thought it was a missile factory. Whether or not they hit their targets, the goal was misery. The Russians were weaponizing winter, and hoping to exhaust both the Ukrainians and the international community.

"The Russians feel like they can move the finish line," Stroh said. "Maybe they peel off some EU members. Maybe these members get tired of the war, of refugees. It behooves neighboring countries to provide Ukraine with weapons," he said, to speed up the conclusion of the war.

For those Ukrainians who had returned, or who had never left, the United States was helping to create sturdier access to power, heat, water, ATMs. Stroh wanted these essentials to exist within what he called "fortresses of unbreakableness"—hardened against missile attacks. Much of this durability work was done through USAID, the American humanitarian-aid agency now run by Samantha Power. By December, the United States had provided $13 billion in direct support that, among other things, had been paying the salaries of Ukrainian government staff, including teachers and hospital workers.

Much of the reason Ukraine is functioning at such a high level in the middle of an existential struggle is this support. The Ukrainian currency is stable, salaries are being paid, and the economy is startlingly robust for a nation under relentless attack. But for how long? So many people in Ukraine asked this question, so I asked Stroh.

"I can't think about that," he said.

I asked about the Patriot missile system, and to my surprise he tipped his hand. By not ruling it out, he implied—to me, at least—that the system, which knocks missiles out of the air with other missiles, would soon be provided to the Ukrainian military. This was a significant step, and a crucial element in defending Ukraine from Russian air attacks. A few days later, this move was announced to the world, provoking loud condemnation from Russia. This was at a stage of the war when every new Western weapon added to the Ukrainian arsenal provoked loud condemnation from the Kremlin, and vague threats of escalation on their part—they continued to whisper about deploying tactical nuclear weapons and/or triggering World War III—but they did nothing along those lines. Instead, they continued to fight on the streets and in trenches, and to periodically send missiles to nonmilitary targets all over Ukraine.

Which did nothing to weaken the Ukrainian resolve.

Back in Kyiv, on our last night in Ukraine, Peter and I went to a candlelight concert. I'd seen the event advertised on a "What to Do in Kyiv" website, and bought tickets for about ten dollars. The crowd was far more glamorous than seemed possible. People arrived, drank wine and tea in the lobby, and milled into the cozy concert hall, where hundreds of battery-powered candles were arranged on the stage. They took pictures in front of the display, then found their seats. It had the feel of a holiday rite—golden and reverent and subdued.

The concert featured a violinist and a pianist, both women, who played ten or so classical standards, but of course nothing Russian. Earlier in the night, Peter had made the comparison to Britain and Ireland. As between Britain and Ireland, between Russia and Ukraine there are innumerable cultural and linguistic and personal interweavings—so many that the two nations could never be wholly separate or wholly different—but that did not mean they were not distinct. That did not mean that the colonial nations of Ukraine and Ireland could be anything but independent and self-determining. And as in Ireland's relationship to Britain, the crimes of the past would never be forgotten by Ukraine. They would be set aside in the name of commerce or family connections, but there would be, for centuries to come, a barely suppressed rage.

At the concert, a group of twentysomethings in the back row made too much noise and were shushed. A pair of maybe-models in front of us, hair pulled tight, watched the concert through masterfully outlined eyes. A few children slumped in their chairs, but most of the audience sat upright, clapped heartily, and, afterward, walked back through the softly falling snow to their apartments and homes, which might or might not be heated that night. Their faces were unworried.

On the way back to the hotel, I stopped outside the Zoloti Vorota, a re-creation of Constantinople's Golden Gate, where a busker was playing a Ukrainian rock song in the dark. The snow fell like ashes as he played alone in the courtyard, with the occasional late-night commuter walking briskly by, hands in coat pockets. I put some rubles in the busker's empty guitar box, where melting snow shared space with a few bills and coins, and CDs for sale.

I took a position on the other side of the square, and soon a man of about thirty approached. He wore no hat, no gloves. His thin brown hair was matted across his forehead.

"You like this music?" he asked.

I said I did.

He wore a tan coat and jeans. He had a beer can in his hand, and smelled like he'd had a few already. He asked where I was from. When I told him, he grimaced.

"I studied business," he said. "My English... I try."

He said his name was Stanislav.

A different man approached Stanislav. Stanislav sent him away with a stiff arm and a string of hissed words.

"Hobo," Stanislav said to me. "You have this word, *hobo*?"

His fetid breath cut through the frozen air. I told him it was an old word, but yes, I knew this word. We stood for a moment in the drifting snow.

"I am from Mariupol," Stanislav said. "You know Mariupol?"

I told him I had read about Mariupol. I pictured row after row of apartment buildings burned black. I assumed the city was now empty.

"My grandparents are in Mariupol," he said. "They won't leave. I beg them on my knees to leave"—he put his ungloved hands in a praying position—"but they won't leave. They say this is their home, blah, blah, blah."

The busker finished his Ukrainian song and began "Last Christmas" by Wham! I told Stanislav I had to leave, that I was taking a train to Poland that night.

"So you leave?" he asked. He looked at the busker and his empty guitar case. "So you leave."

The train left Kyiv at eleven. When Peter and I got to the four-bed compartment we'd been assigned, we found two young men occupying the bottom bunks. They were Ukrainian soldiers in uniform, both of them teenagers. They smiled at us.

The smell was outrageous. These teenagers hadn't showered in some time, it seemed clear, and it was likely they had been wrestling with each other just before we got there. Peter and I threw our bags onto the upper bunks and settled in.

The train was old, Soviet-era, its every surface steel and painted mauve.

Outside, the temperature was dropping to zero, but as we left Kyiv, the train car's heat kicked in and soon we were traveling in a kind of rolling womb—hot and rocking steadily, redolent with human stench.

The soldiers below sat side by side on one of the beds, giggling as they watched videos on their phones. They were at once obnoxious and extremely polite, and I was glad they were headed away from the fighting, not toward it. They snorted, and wrestled some more, and it seemed they would never be quiet. But as midnight approached, they settled in and took their separate beds, but they did not sleep. They were likely going home on leave, and were too happy to rest.

Peter was already asleep, and just as I was drifting off, I heard a loud rapping on the floor. Seconds later the soldier below me tapped my shoulder. His unblemished face was grinning. "Yours," he said. He'd retrieved a pair of coins that had fallen from my pocket and onto the floor. I thanked him, and he and I resumed our places. Ten minutes later it happened again. Again he gathered the fallen coins and stood and returned them to me. "Yours," he said again. This time I took all the contents of my pockets and stashed them in my backpack. I fell asleep without a blanket. It had gotten tropical inside, even as frost overtook the windows, even as the speed of the train, a Soviet relic, seemed untenable. Through the night some shake or rattle woke me briefly, and always the two soldiers were there, lying awake, side by side, until they weren't. At some frozen station in the dark, they'd gotten off, and two women, a mother and grown daughter, had gotten on. They whispered cheerfully as we woke in the pearly dawn, hurtling inexorably west. ★

A portion of this essay first appeared in The New Yorker.

ANIMAL

RUMI

by Azareen Van der Vliet Oloomi

FEATURES:

★ 1,200 pounds

★ 16.1 hands tall

★ Seven years old

★ Acquired in 2022

★ American Azteca, bred from Andalusians and American Quarter Horses

This is the ephemeral side of the universe and Rumi stands at its center. Mythological. Supreme. Noble. Defensive. The highest-ranking member of the herd.

He smells of herbs and soaked pebbles and dried mud, of a wet nascent earth, and his silver coat glows at night with the refracted light of the moon. Time swivels and swerves in his large charcoal eyes. Nothing gets past him. He is sensorium supreme. He is elixir, cure-all, excelsior. To keep his herd safe, he scans herd and hearth, remote hills and backwoods.

At dusk Rumi saunters through plumes of steam that come off the cooling land, his legs wrapped in a gauzy mist. He has a job to do: to protect the elderly bay from the Norwegian Fjord, fat and squat with a punk's hedgehog for a mane.

The Fjord has a habit of crowding the ancient, thinning Thoroughbred during feeding time. The Thoroughbred has seen better days. He was cheered for years on the racetracks by extravagant ladies with feathered hats who bet on his fate. Now here he is, an old man relying on Rumi to protect his position along the hay line—Rumi, a mere yearling, a boy with the arrogance of a prince.

Rumi jerks his head up in the Fjord's direction. He keeps his eyes on that wide-bodied, bloated punk of a horse! Rumi's eyelids are creased and tense, his lips tightly sealed, his nostrils flared and stretched thin to insinuate the brewing of a confident neigh.

He has assumed the posture of a stallion, as if he were still entire. The Fjord cuts his losses and clears out. But it's too late. Rumi is all rage at the Fjord's defective judgment, his total lack of grace. He charges at him.

The Fjord's eyes widen as he takes in Rumi's perfectly sloping shoulders and long legs and broad croup; his free, dancing trot; his hooves that kick out in pleasure as though all of life were a game—the bull a game! the cow a game! the smell of death approaching in the air a game!—to be faced with flare. Rumi cuts the dirt and delivers a high kick to the Fjord. He imprints his hoof on the Fjord's hindquarter to underscore his point: *Mind your place!*

When all is said and done, Rumi shakes out his mane and stands with his hind legs splayed and with his gaze pins the Fjord in his place at the end of the hay line near the rusting troughs. He likes to celebrate his victories, come hell or high water! He nods his big silver head and lifts one leg to paw at the earth. He is satisfied. He licks and chews. Hot sighs of relief come barreling out of his nostrils. But his mood turns on a dime. He becomes severe, pensive. A tremor travels down his flank.

The horses, attuned to his shifts, jerk their heads up as one. They stand at attention as Rumi surveys the land. He is majestic. Shiny as marble and touched along his nose and mane and tail and knobby knees by the smoke of fire. He scans the earth. An encroaching ambush? Tense seconds, long as the universe, go by. Nothing. It was only the sky speaking its language, crackling away. Electricity working itself out over the jagged mountains.

Rumi lowers his head to the feed. His arched mane darkens from the shadow of the earth. The herd goes back to grazing and all is calm in the draping night. No idle chatter, no stowed bitterness, no divisive speech.

At dawn, the strange motley affair of life will begin. Rumi, ever eager, will rise before the others to take his place at the helm. The sun will bring its heat down on his muscular neck, and he will parade beneath the stars and planets that circle him. "Rumi, our peaceful warrior!" the birded trees will sing! ★

Illustration by Eden Weingart

EULA BISS

[WRITER]

"MY LONG-TERM INTEREST IS IN THE FORCES
THAT THREATEN HUMAN CONNECTION."

The evolving thoughts Eula Biss had while rereading a challenging work of auto-ethnography:
"I hate this book."
"This book is terrible."
"One doesn't read a book one hates three times."

To read Eula Biss's work is to watch a writer doing the hard work of disassembling American mythologies in light of the facts. Her essays are shot through with an unflinching examination of our own self-narrated identities, as they relate to marriage, family, racism, vaccination, class, capitalism, debt, and property. In The Balloonists *(Hanging Loose Press, 2002), she explores the dissolution of a marriage. In* Notes from No Man's Land: American Essays *(Graywolf Press, 2009), which won the National Book Critics Circle Award, she plumbs the fictions of whiteness. In* On Immunity: An Inoculation *(Graywolf Press, 2014), she investigates the anxieties and metaphors around vaccination. In* Having and Being *Had (Riverhead Books, 2020), she writes through the dumbing effect of capitalism's distortions to examine how we value labor, art, and one another. She is currently at work on her next book, about private property.*

Illustration by Kristian Hammerstad

In all her work, Biss scrutinizes the nature of our connection in American life. In one of her early essays, "Time and Distance Overcome," she looks at how telephone poles, instruments of communication, became gallows in public lynchings across the country in the early twentieth century. Vaccines— our greatest collective defense against viral disease—become a symbol of violation and trespass. Money, our shared concrete metaphor of value, becomes a tool of exclusion. Each subject Biss examines exposes the contested ground on which we make and remake our American identities.

It isn't easy to see one's own story on a collision course with the facts. I recently re-read Biss's essay "Goodbye to All That," about leaving New York and youthful misperceptions. In Joan Didion's essay by the same name, she recalls an unfurnished apartment where she hung gold curtains, hoping the warm color would make her feel better. Instead, they blew out in a tangle and were ruined by the rain. Biss also puts up curtains to hide an empty room. By now we know the reference. The stories we tell ourselves are window dressing.

Biss and I have long shared work as friends, but for her most recent manuscript, she hired me to work with her through the final stages of revision. Though I am familiar with Biss's subjects and her uncompromising acuity, Having and Being Had *presented new challenges for me as an editor and for her as a writer. The pacing and tonal register were new territory for Biss, as was the conceptual heart of the project—capitalism and alienated labor. It eventually became clear that* Having and Being Had *was a natural next step in Biss's oeuvre. On two occasions, we sat down via Zoom and talked about how she approached each of her books and the overarching inquiries that have motivated her.*

—Mara Naselli

I. THE MARRIAGE OF MISSION AND STYLE

THE BELIEVER: Each book you write is distinct stylistically, as if you are working to figure out how your medium will best serve a particular subject. How does each project make its demands on you?

EULA BISS: Yes, each book makes different demands, and the part that's exciting and challenging, from a craft point of view, is figuring out what has to happen stylistically. What are the stylistic requirements of this particular subject matter or this particular project? Who do I have to be as a writer to make this happen?

That question results in works that are fairly stylistically distinct. I have always been preoccupied with how I can bend this medium to my purposes. I wrote my first book, *The Balloonists*, while I was supposed to be writing my undergraduate thesis, which I intended to be a big, serious work of nonfiction about marriage. I was doing lots of research and making zero progress on that thesis. The only thing I had written were these notes to myself, fragments of memory and experience, all loosely associated with the problem of marriage.

I couldn't yet see this as a legitimate way of writing, though it was my way. This was how I talked to myself privately, on the side, but I thought that if I was going to make a public document, I would have to do it the way other people did it. When I allowed myself to let go of that, my notes became *The Balloonists*.

The breakthrough for me in that book was in embracing an unconventional stylistic and formal approach that felt organic to my thinking and my subject. But I still made some effort to write according to the conventions of genre, and those efforts failed. The only book manuscript I've never published was written immediately after *The Balloonists* and pursued questions posed by that book: What if we discard our received narratives about marriage? What if we reinvent the institution for our own needs? What would marriage look like if its purpose was to serve relationships between people, rather than all the other historical purposes it has served, like consolidating wealth, and making property out of women?

That unpublished manuscript was a bid to be taken seriously as a writer. I had been writing between genres, publishing prose poetry, working in a space that was marginal, and I wanted to be understood as a serious writer. I thought, OK, I'm going to have to speak the language that people take seriously. So I'll step aside from my playful engagement with the boundary between poetry and prose and I'll write a straight-ahead work based on journalistic techniques. That book failed in part because there was a disconnect between what the book was saying and the way it was written.

That manuscript was about queering marriage—I guess that might be the best way of saying it. This was in the early aughts, when gay marriage was all over the news. But the way the question of gay marriage was being framed was: Should the government allow gay people to enter this sacred institution? Will it ruin marriage if we let gay people in? My argument was more like, we'd better ruin it—we've got to break it to save it.

That argument was too strange for the very straight-ahead stylistic approach I chose—there was a mismatch between the mission and the style. I wasn't letting myself write about unconventional marriages in an unconventional style; I was trying to force myself to be the serious writer I wanted people to think I was.

BLVR: What were your stylistic strategies in *Notes from No Man's Land*?

EB: I was writing *Notes* simultaneous to working on that marriage manuscript. Those essays were an outlet for me to write the way I really wanted to write, the way I felt comfortable writing. That work was a place where I could develop my skills in handling, say, a fractured text that offered a kaleidoscopic look at a question or a problem. But again, this was my side project. It still didn't feel totally legitimate, and that wasn't just in my head. The response I would sometimes get from editors when I sent them work was, "What is this?"

At that time, the kind of essays I was writing were still on the far margins of what was accepted as nonfiction. That's no longer true, and one of the strange experiences of my career arc is that I have mostly stayed in an experimental relationship with my prose, abandoning conventions when I need to, but the kind of writing I do has become increasingly mainstream. Claudia Rankine's *Citizen: An American Lyric* and Leslie Jamison's *The Empathy Exams*, Maggie Nelson's *The Argonauts*—their success with readers brought a way of writing that had been happening in the margins into the mainstream. Claudia had been doing that kind of writing for a long time. *Don't Let Me Be Lonely: An American Lyric* was a book I admired in grad school. Hilton Als was also doing genre-bending work. *The Women* was hugely influential on me in college. When I read that book I thought, This is what I want to do! He was combining literary criticism, sociology, personal narrative, autobiography, biography—drawing widely

from all these different modes and approaches and making his own work, which was a response to his own questions and ideas. That was exciting to me.

BLVR: One of the most interesting things in re-reading *Notes from No Man's Land* was the notes, which function as a shadow text, tracing one thread of inquiry to the next. There's a mainstream idea, particularly around the personal essay, that the essayistic mode is breezy and impressionistic. But these notes show a rigorous undergirding of research and thinking.

EB: That notes section in *Notes from No Man's Land* was inspired by Claudia Rankine's *Don't Let Me Be Lonely*. When I hit the notes in that book, I thought, Oh, I've got to go back and read this book again. The notes were what signaled to me that the book was doing something more complicated than I had originally understood.

The word *notes* in the title of *Notes from No Man's Land* is an homage to James Baldwin, but *notes* is also my word for the private conversation I have with myself on the page. In *Notes from No Man's Land*, I developed that private conversation into a public document. I was talking to myself, but I was also talking to history. I was propelled by the urgent necessity to better understand my race in this historical context. What does it mean to be white in this country now?

I lived in New York City when I started writing that book, and it was palpable to me that my race meant something to the people around me. I could see that. I felt it in interactions. I had this unsettling sense that all these people around me seemed to understand something about me that I didn't understand about myself. I felt like, OK, I can't continue to be dumber about whiteness than everyone around me.

BLVR: In *Notes* you take up the mandate Baldwin puts to whites early in his career: Save yourselves. Save your own soul. None of this is going to get better until you recognize you're not winning.

EB: Yes, exactly.

BLVR: Since both *No Man's Land* and *On Immunity*, we've had a revival of white nationalism and a pandemic heavily politicized over vaccination.

EB: I've always believed that I can't write timely work, because I'm such a slow writer. The one book I didn't publish was going to be my timely book, written in response to the debate over gay marriage. If my work is prescient in any way, it's because I write from the questions that feel most pressing in my everyday lived life. Because I'm a product of this culture, things that feel pressing to me are often things that feel that way to other people. But it takes some time for the things that feel pressing in our everyday lives to become a public conversation. *On Immunity* did not look like a major book when I began work on it. At that time, my subject looked small and unnecessary, domestic and gendered. But the question of vaccination felt huge in my everyday life. This question was tearing apart communities of new mothers, but the national discourse hadn't caught up yet, for reasons I think are sexist.

BLVR: To be honest, when you told me you were writing a book on vaccination, I thought, *What?* Certainly that prejudice was embedded in my response.

EB: I didn't even take vaccination that seriously. At first I didn't want to write a book—I just wanted to write an essay. The subject kept spilling over the bounds of a single essay.

II. THE SHAPE OF THOUGHT

BLVR: What about the stylistic demands of *On Immunity*? That book has a very different voice from *Notes from No Man's Land*. It's more discursive.

EB: That more discursive quality came directly from the pressures of my material. As I learned more about my subject matter, I saw more clearly that part of what was going on behind many people's fears of vaccination, including my own, was very loose associative thinking, which I recognized because I'm an associative thinker. The shape of my work up until that point was usually dictated by association, my most comfortable mode of thought. Over the course of researching that book, I made the dreadful realization—I was going to have to write a book that critiqued the way of thinking that was most natural for me.

I investigated various loose associations around vaccination, like the idea that the financial corruption of big pharmaceutical companies is corrupting the purity of vaccines. I came to see that, actually, the evidence doesn't point to that. My research led me again and again to the understanding that these associations might make sense to me and might be, in many ways, legitimate associations, but they don't lead to truths. It was a horrible thing for me to realize. The whole book became an exercise in critiquing my own style of thought. The actual writing was painful. It hurt. It hurt my brain. I was working against my own impulses as a thinker and constantly checking myself and constantly forcing myself to rewind an association and think it through and logically parse it out. It was psychologically and creatively exhausting. When I finished that book, I felt good about it, felt proud of it, felt I had really pushed myself and made myself write in a way that wasn't comfortable for me. And I also felt like I never wanted to do that again.

BLVR: It made you sick.

EB: Yeah. It brought me to my knees. So the permission I gave myself when I finished *On Immunity* was to let myself do whatever I felt like doing in the next book. Let it be associative, let it be poetry, let it be whatever. This book was real work, so the next one's going to be play.

BLVR: And funny.

EB: As it turns out, *Having and Being Had* was real work too. Also painful. But it started as play, with me messing around and making jokes. And I allowed myself to return to wide associations.

BLVR: It's a remarkable insight for you to discover that associative thinking could not govern the form of *On Immunity*.

EB: *On Immunity* was actually about the shape thought takes. It was as much about metaphor as it was about vaccination. That book demanded that I interrogate what metaphor is, how it's working in our discourses, and how it's working on a very personal level. I had to examine the metaphors that we use in our own minds for what we're doing when we inject something into our bodies. Is that a violation? What metaphors does the penetration of skin invite? For a lot of people, that invites rape metaphors. Rape, sexual violence, physical violence, and state violence come up again and again in conversations about vaccination. It's a powerful metaphorical space.

Working with metaphor was one of my inheritances from poetry—from being trained by poets, from reading poetry, from being in community with poets, from writing poetry. My relationship with metaphor was then deepened and complicated in writing *On Immunity*. I had to regard metaphor as a tool, rather than just using it. I had to ask: How is this tool best used? I entered *Having and Being Had* with a much more sophisticated understanding of how I wanted to use metaphor and how it's responsibly employed. And what its dangers are too.

I didn't want to go into writing about capitalism with a knee-jerk, unexamined attitude that capitalism is just bad, whatever it is. That's why that book has this refrain: "What is capitalism?" I didn't want to let myself critique something I couldn't even define.

III. THE PLIABILITY OF METAPHORS

BLVR: In your work you consistently show how pliable our interpretations of metaphors can be. Metaphor can lead us to define ourselves against others. Or it can lead us to understand how deeply interconnected we are.

EB: Yes.

BLVR: Plato wanted to get rid of poets because poets have the ability to ignite the passions and compel us to abandon our reason. I love that your books, using the tools of the poet and the tools of reason, bring a thinking, feeling pressure to urgent and emotionally volatile questions.

EB: Yes. Feeling is a kind of thinking, and thinking often comes from feeling. That tension you noted in *On Immunity* around connectedness and disconnectedness—as you've observed, that's a through line across all my work. Every book I've written is about relationships between people and the ways those relationships are threatened by institutionalized ideas. My long-term interest is in the forces that threaten human connection.

For me, the most everyday experience of pain around racism is the way it damages relationships and makes certain kinds of relationships impossible or improbable. Even the people who seem to be benefiting materially from racism are losing relationships with other people and losing a depth of relation and a richness of relation.

I didn't think about that until you brought it up—this thread through all the books—but one of my primary investments in writing about racism is trying to recognize and understand the damage that's done interpersonally. And also to reclaim the possibilities. As with marriage. There's an institutionalized idea of what marriage is, and we have to work around that idea. In a racialized society, we've got to somehow figure out how to be in relationship with one another outside of the damaging, destructive concept of racial superiority.

IV. INOCULATION AGAINST FORGETFULNESS

BLVR: There is a relational inquiry underway in *Having and Being Had* around money and class. This book is so formally and tonally distinct from your previous books. How did you approach this manuscript?

EB: At first, I just wrote and watched what was happening. After doing some preliminary, exploratory writing, I knew the book would be composed of short, titled pieces written in the present tense. This lashed me to the moment in which I was writing. The book was about money and class, and I had more money in that moment than I'd ever had in the past. My strong inclination was to retreat into the past, where I'd had less money, to hide in a situation that felt more comfortable on the page.

Many of the rules I imposed on my own writing in this book were about not allowing myself to hide. In one piece I recount a conversation with my sister where I tell her that I haven't bought a house so much as I've bought a $400,000 container for a washing machine—I'm kind of joking and kind of serious. When I revisited that conversation on the page, I saw that I had rounded down considerably. The actual cost of the house was $485,000, so really, I should have rounded up to $500,000. I had to ask myself why I had lied to my own sister. The answer was because I felt self-conscious.

I was aware that my sister had paid about half that price for her house. I knew who I was talking to. I did the thing many of us in the middle class do when we're talking to another member of the middle class who's in a different housing market or a different income bracket—we adjust the facts of our own life slightly. I did that without really thinking about it. So I made a rule for myself that there would be no more of that.

I had projects in this book that were private, as well as public projects. For the reader, I wanted to explore and expose middle-class complicity. For my own private project, it was really important to me that the narrator not be disingenuous.

It took me a while to understand the tone or posture that emerged in this book, a tone that was somewhat relaxed and light and fairly sardonic. This was a different tone for me. As I watched the work unfold, I understood that making an earnest or self-serious critique of class and capitalism felt disingenuous to me.

BLVR: And would be absurd.

EB: Yes! To be honest, I had to be making fun of myself. And yet, I'm serious about my own conviction that there are

═══════════════════════════

MICROINTERVIEW WITH WO CHAN, PART IV

THE BELIEVER: There's a sequence of poems in the collection that are all in the second person. Could you talk about those?

WO CHAN: I wrote those second-person prose poems in 2014 and 2015. I remember I was reading Claudia Rankine's books *Citizen* and *Don't Let Me Be Lonely*—so they are deeply influenced by her work—but at the time I was also just really obsessed with watching *Chopped*. I had recently moved to New York, and I think it was comforting to watch people work in a kitchen, the environment in which I grew up. I'd also go to Chinatown for dinner and listen to the sound of stainless steel trays hitting stainless steel tables and people speaking in Fuzhou dialect. If I closed my eyes, suddenly I'd be eight years old again. In that kind of moment it feels like another voice is talking about me or at me through the atmosphere. That's what the second person feels like to me. ✶

no winners in this unjust system. I feel the same way about whiteness—social hierarchies are mutually destructive to those at the top and the bottom. I'm dead serious about that.

Years ago the novelist Lê Thị Diễm Thúy described the Vietnamese tea ceremony to me as a writing lesson. The aesthetic of the ceremony is to hold heavy things as if they are very light, to lift a teapot as if it is made of air. And then to hold light things, such as a teacup, as if they are very heavy. This motion, sinking and floating in two different directions, is part of what creates the beauty of the ceremony. That was a lesson on aesthetics I never forgot—it spoke to my sensibility. I have an appreciation for heavy subjects treated as if they're light, and light subjects treated as if they're heavy. I think both things are happening in this book in various ways.

BLVR: It took me a while to figure out how to approach *Having and Being Had* in manuscript.

EB: It was interesting to me that you had to go through that process as a reader. I didn't feel that much ahead of you at that point, even though the book was almost done when I showed the manuscript to you. I had all these questions and misgivings about what was going on in it. There were quite a few elements that I knew had to be a certain way, but I didn't know why. I was just feeling my way through. I came to you in this very trembling state—I thought, It has to be this way, but I don't know why! Help me!

BLVR: I do think works contain their own instruction manuals.

EB: You told me the book would provide the key to read the map. By the time I gave the manuscript to you, I knew it required a lot of interpretive work. I wanted to craft a surface for this book that was pleasurable and easy in a way, to hide my own work as a writer. So much of this book is about different kinds of labor. But it is also about pleasure, and where we find pleasure in work and where we don't. I was enjoying the fact that I was putting a tremendous amount of work into making the book read as if it hadn't demanded all that work.

It's a book that offers the reader both pleasure and work, ideally. You helped me by articulating your own interpretative work as a reader, and by showing me where that work was too much of a strain.

BLVR: I struggled with the manuscript, in part, because I misread it at first as an argument with intellectual history. Then, at 3:00 a.m., after a few passes, the images began to click and I realized it needed to be read as a poem.

EB: Yes, as a poem. With attention to metaphor and suggestion and pattern and repetition. There's a repetition of the word *understanding* in this book. I feared losing a certain kind of understanding by moving into a new economic status. There is an essential knowledge—there's no better word—a knowledge that you acquire through being in constant conversation with people who are financially insecure. I had a visceral fear when I made this move into homeownership that I was going to become out of touch, that I was going to lose some essential, everyday knowledge. There's a common assumption that once you have that knowledge you never lose it. People often announce their class status as the class they grew up in, and the fantasy is that you never lose what you learned from being in that situation. But you can lose what you learned. I felt myself losing it. Knowledge is fragile.

V. THE GIFT ECONOMY

BLVR: Political theorist Danielle Allen has written how, as a country, we have privileged liberty over equality. Yet when we are confronted face-to-face with inequality, we are so ashamed that we lie to ourselves about our own privilege and sheer good luck.

EB: Those lies and that shame are both socially destructive. The particular aspect of capitalism that most interested me in *Having and Being Had* was how capitalism was shaping my relationships with other people. Where was it damaging those relationships? What was it making possible or impossible? That's one reason why the book is saturated with a quiet sense of loss. I experienced real loss alongside material gain. And the two are not unrelated to each other.

There's a quote I love from Fred Moten in his book *The Undercommons: Fugitive Planning and Black Study*: "I don't need your help. I just need you to recognize that this shit is killing you, too, however much more softly, you stupid motherfucker, you know?"

That's how I feel—this shit is killing me too. Terms like *allyship* don't appeal to me because that language implies that you're providing aid in someone else's war. That's not how I think about it. I feel like, no, actually, I'm fighting my own war, for my own sake.

We're the inheritors of a lot of historical—

BLVR: Assumptions?

EB: I wanted to just say *mess*. We've inherited this historical mess that we call whiteness. And this historical mess we call capitalism. This mess is so pervasive in so many parts of my life that I'm not even sure where to locate it.

The question that led to *Having and Being Had* came out of a short chapter in *On Immunity* that's explicitly about capitalism, specifically vampire capitalism. One of the things capitalism is taking from us is our ability to trust other people's motives. If you live in a society where the assumption is that everyone's motives are profit driven, that generates a kind of ambient paranoia, a general lack of trust. When I saw this in anti-vax literature, I began to wonder, What is capitalism doing to us psychologically? How is it hurting our ability to trust each other and interact with each other in productive ways? How is this system shaping my life and my relationships and my own thinking? Are there ideas I can't have because I've absorbed the tenets of capitalism in some fundamental way? Are there possibilities in my life that seem unapproachable because I've absorbed the precepts of capitalism? And the answer was yes. Yes, there are.

Part of the personal work of writing *Having* was undoing some of the assumptions I had absorbed so I could make decisions that looked like bad decisions according to the logic of capitalism, but that were the right decisions for me. I had to really talk myself through the question: What is capitalism doing to my mind?

I'm increasingly interested in this intersection between things that are real—like interactions with other people—and powerful concepts that are essentially imaginary. Race is conceptual, but it's a reality in our everyday lives. Racism does real damage. And it's an idea, an imaginary idea.

What ultimately brought me to writing about land as property, which will be my next book and is the companion book to *Having and Being Had*, is that property, like race, is conceptual. One of Robert Nichols's central points in *Theft*

Is Property!: Dispossession and Critical Theory is that the idea of land as property is wholly conceptual. Land is real and you can occupy land and have a relationship with land as a person. But once you step into the idea of owning land, you're in an entirely conceptual space. The ownership of land isn't real, in that sense. David Graeber argues that property relationships are really relationships with other people. We're not talking about our relationship with a thing when we talk about owning property. We're talking about the rules we are making about how we can interact with each other. He writes, "Property is a social relation... [that] consists of the right to exclude 'all the world' from access to a certain house, or shirt, or piece of land." Private property is one person saying, *Here's what you other people can't do.* Not *Here's my relationship to this thing.*

BLVR: In *Having*, the search to rethink the value of connection and art-making functions as an antidote to the predatory effects of the marketplace.

EB: Art-making and parenting are similar in that way. They are both antidotes to the market in part because they hold little economic value. We don't parent for profit. And most artists make art at a loss.

BLVR: And yet both parenting and art-making can be undone by the perceived and actual pressures of the market economy. It is difficult to understand the value of art if we take the market to be its primary measure. It wasn't until I read *The Gift: How the Creative Spirit Transforms the World* by Lewis Hyde that I could finally see that art-making and the market are at odds. The disposition best suited to art-making is the logic of the fairy tale, not the logic of the balance sheet.

EB: What's beautiful about this is that *The Gift* is a book you gave me! It's emblematic to me of the gifts that are passed between artists in community with each other. There's an informal system among artists of supporting each other, supporting each other's work, reading for each other, as you and I have read for each other, and providing all these necessary services. It's not just editing each other and critiquing each other. It's also providing each other with the sense that what we're doing matters, which is essential if you live in a system where your work doesn't matter unless it earns money.

As I was working on *Having*, I came to the decision that I would sell the book to buy myself time to write. And I did. I sold it for more money than everything I'd earned as a writer for the whole twenty years of my writing career that preceded this book. Making money off a capitalist critique within a capitalist system felt subversive and at the same time the opposite of subversive—emblematic of what I get to do with the position I'm in. The book is full of contradictions and both parts of this particular contradiction are true. There's true subversion in what I did with the book and it's also a true manifestation of privilege.

I recently read an interview with the painter Julie Mehretu. She was commissioned to do a mural for Goldman Sachs, and she put some thought into why she would take a commission from this huge financial institution. She had her reasons and they were artistic—it was going to be the biggest work she'd ever created and she had ambitions that were going to be made possible by this commission. She said all this without apology. I liked her clarity. Her clarity of purpose was about serving her vision as an artist. If a bank was going to give her five million dollars to execute her vision, then as an artist, she was going to take it.

BLVR: To serve the work.

EB: Yes. Which brings us back to *The Gift*. Questions about capitalism throughout *Having* are overt. What is less overt is that I'm also thinking about generosity and gifts and informal economies. As much as I'm critiquing certain elements of capitalism, I'm celebrating the true generosity that I encounter in my daily life. I've been the beneficiary of so much generosity. The book opens with a list of all the things that people in my apartment building in Chicago gave to me—those material things stand in for the sense of generous community I enjoyed there. I also enjoy that kind of community among artists. Part of why the book is filled with these little exchanges with other artists and other writers, including you, is that I'm celebrating the richness these exchanges bring to my life—exchanges with people who are generous intellectually, who share their ideas and push my ideas and see where I'm going with my thinking and then support that thinking by, say, giving me the book *The Gift*. You sent me on this trajectory that turned into a major project for me.

As I wrote *Having and Being Had*, I thought about how the book could be generous. One of the generosities, as I see it, is that I made all my critiques through myself.

BLVR: You give the reader a way to look at a system intimate to our own lives. To examine one's own situation is threatening and scary. There's so much ink spilled about the limits of the first-person narrator, the limits of the personal essay, but this is an example of how high those stakes can be.

EB: That's what I want it to be. I'm a believer in the plural first person, the first person who stands in for a whole class or set of people. Most first-person speakers are not speaking for everyone, but they might be speaking for a group. I'm offering a mirror, and if the reader has certain things in common with me, that mirror is going to create a complicated reading experience. Some readers are ready and eager to look into the mirror, and some will want to look away.

BLVR: There's a mastery to drawing a reader into doubting her own mythologies. It's the reader's choice to stay with her own confusion, unsettledness, discomfort.

EB: I learned a lot about how my book probably feels to readers by reading *My Life with Things*, by Elizabeth Chin. As an anthropologist, she studied consumption and the consumption habits of poor people of color in Connecticut. But in this book, she decided to turn the same tools on herself, a university professor, and to take field notes on her life. Initially, I read it and thought, I hate this book. This book is terrible. I found it disturbing, but I wasn't ready to admit to myself why. Then I read it again, and a third time. Then I thought, One doesn't read a book one hates three times.

BLVR: That's the gift economy at work—working on you in ways you're not engineering, ways that are not merely reinforcing views or feelings you already have. In fairy tales there is often a bid to engagement, and sometimes these relationships are scary or even dangerous. A crow or a bear or an old woman asks something of you, and the journey begins. You don't know where you will go, but you know you will be transformed, as long as you don't deny the bid. In *The Gift*, Hyde writes, "The

passage into mystery always refreshes. If… we can look once a day upon the face of mystery, then our labor satisfies."

EB: That's the gift of literature—it's transformation, but it's transformation you have to participate in. It's not the touch of a wand; it's much more like the contract with an old woman and the labors. There are often labors in fairy tales, a series of labors or tests, and the transformation is enacted after those labors, or through those labors. I think the works that have offered me the most radical transformation are works that were very difficult for me—not hard to read for formal reasons, but difficult because it was hard to hear what they were saying. ✶

MICROINTERVIEW WITH WO CHAN, PART V

THE BELIEVER: As an early reader of your work, I've noticed your enduring attraction to the disgusting and the repulsive. I wondered if you could talk more about how you are drawn to that material.

WO CHAN: Many of my earliest memories involve repulsive things—or maybe they're just what I choose to remember. For example, my relationship to cockroaches: Growing up in a restaurant, I was trained that if I saw a roach, I would go into Terminator mode. As subtly as possible, I would walk up to it in front of a dining room full of patrons and step on it. Once, when I was still in China and living in this one-bedroom apartment with my brothers and my mom, I was playing in the kitchen and I pulled out a screw from underneath the table, and a cascade of roaches fell onto my face. It was terrifying. Ten years later, now in the United States, there was an era in our restaurant life when we were constantly fighting the roaches. One time we got shut down. That was the only vacation we ever took, when the health inspector shut us down. We splurged on a new type of roach killer, and for months there would be straggling roaches, bleeding out, dazed and confused. So there was a recurring vileness. But I think, as a queer person, I could accept this. Bodies are bodies and we have to accept them. Nature is nature and we have to be a part of it. ✶

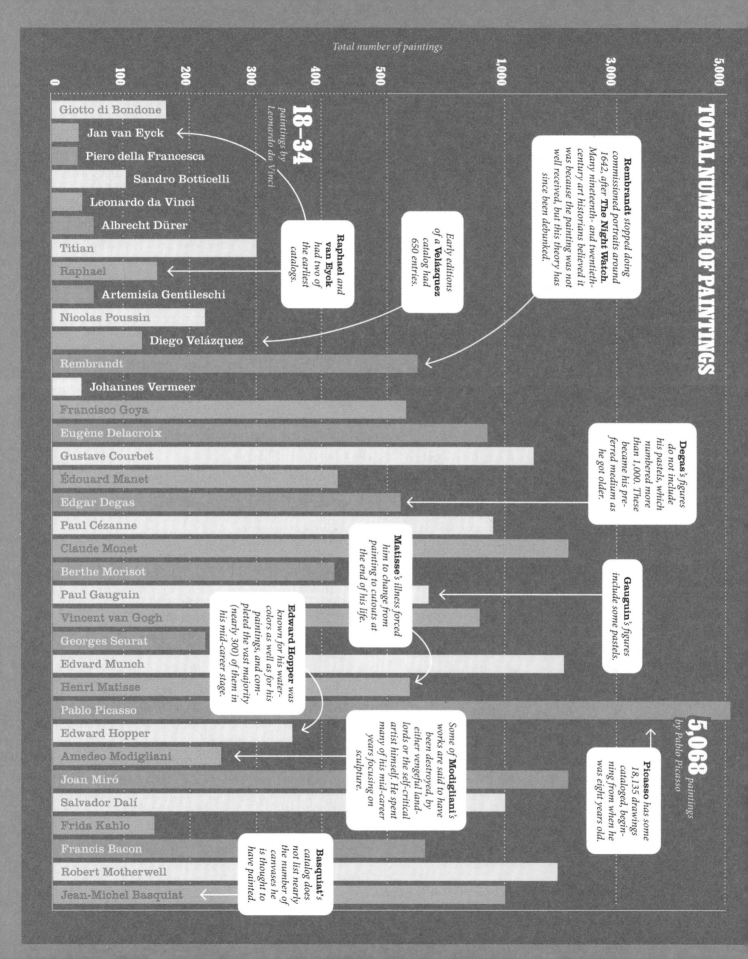

TOTAL NUMBER OF PAINTINGS

Total number of paintings

0   100   200   300   400   500   1,000   3,000   5,000

Giotto di Bondone

Jan van Eyck

Piero della Francesca

Sandro Botticelli

Leonardo da Vinci

Albrecht Dürer

Titian

Raphael

Artemisia Gentileschi

Nicolas Poussin

Diego Velázquez

Rembrandt

Johannes Vermeer

Francisco Goya

Eugène Delacroix

Gustave Courbet

Édouard Manet

Edgar Degas

Paul Cézanne

Claude Monet

Berthe Morisot

Paul Gauguin

Vincent van Gogh

Georges Seurat

Edvard Munch

Henri Matisse

Pablo Picasso

Edward Hopper

Amedeo Modigliani

Joan Miró

Salvador Dalí

Frida Kahlo

Francis Bacon

Robert Motherwell

Jean-Michel Basquiat

18–34
Paintings by
Leonardo da Vinci

5,068
by Pablo Picasso

Rembrandt stopped doing commissioned portraits around 1642, after **The Night Watch**. Many nineteenth- and twentieth-century art historians believed it was because the painting was not well received, but this theory has since been debunked.

Raphael and **van Eyck** had two of the earliest catalogs.

Early editions of a **Velázquez** catalog had 650 entries.

Degas's figures do not include his pastels, which numbered more than 1,000. These became his preferred medium as he got older.

Gauguin's figures include some pastels.

Matisse's illness forced him to change from painting to cutouts at the end of his life.

Edward Hopper was known for his watercolors as well as for his paintings, and completed the vast majority (nearly 300) of them in his mid-career stage.

Some of **Modigliani**'s works are said to have been destroyed, by either vengeful landlords or the self-critical artist himself. He spent many of his mid-career years focusing on sculpture.

Picasso has some 18,135 drawings cataloged, beginning from when he was eight years old.

Basquiat's catalog does not list nearly the number of canvases he is thought to have painted.

PAINT BY NUMBERS

by Ginger Greene

Catalogues raisonnés, or critical catalogs, first emerged in the mid-seventeenth century as a way of documenting an artist's entire body of work. From the outset, they were a fraught product. Commonly authored by dealers and collectors who benefitted from authenticating certain works, they were beholden to commercial interests. Yet today these catalogs are our best tool for tracking the output of many historic artists. They are strange documents, full of cryptic symbols, complex naming conventions, and (oft-contested) publishing histories. They change with each new edition and often contradict themselves. They are esoteric and, in some cases, extremely expensive. And yet they are also highly compelling; each one a judicious attempt to archive the totality of an artist's unruly, partial, or damaged body of work. I have relied on them here to estimate the rates at which certain major artists produced work. Of course, these numbers are approximations and may be revised over time.

#	ARTIST NAME	YEARS	TOTAL PAINTINGS	OUTPUT RATE PER WORKING YEAR	EARLY CAREER	MID-CAREER	LATE CAREER
1	Giotto di Bondone	1267–1377	136–175	0.2	64	61	25
2	Jan van Eyck	1390–1441	19–34	1.2	6	18	16
3	Piero della Francesca	1416–1492	20–33	0.63	9	15	9
4	Sandro Botticelli	1444–1510	110	2.6	59	51	44
5	Leonardo da Vinci	1452–1519	18–34	0.5	12	10	9
6	Albrecht Dürer	1471–1528	55	1.4	19	19	17
7	Titian	1476–1576	300	4.3	82	98	90
8	Raphael	1483–1520	156	6	27	72	57
9	Artemisia Gentileschi	1593–1653	53	1.2	14	26	13
10	Nicolas Poussin	1594–1665	231	5.5	109	85	31
11	Diego Velázquez	1599–1660	129	3	58	42	29
12	Rembrandt	1606–1669	340–611	10.3	169	67	88
13	Johannes Vermeer	1632–1675	35	2.1	18	10	7
14	Francisco Goya	1746–1828	556	10.2	166	287	103
15	Eugène Delacroix	1798–1863	921	19.6	221	284	305
16	Gustave Courbet	1819–1877	1,500	34.1	89	724	246
17	Édouard Manet	1832–1883	430	13.4	73	145	212
18	Edgar Degas	1834–1917	521	9.6	244	140	133
19	Paul Cézanne	1839–1906	954	19.9	237	462	255
20	Claude Monet	1840–1926	2,050	29.7	968	627	408
21	Berthe Morisot	1841–1895	423	11.4	274	120	22
22	Paul Gauguin	1848–1903	638	19.3	65	431	142
23	Vincent van Gogh	1853–1890	871	87.1	92	356	406
24	Georges Seurat	1859–1891	220	16.9	62	119	30
25	Edvard Munch	1863–1944	2,000	31.3	500	958	331
26	Henri Matisse	1869–1954	538	8.3	171	312	54
27	Pablo Picasso	1881–1973	5,068	63.4	1321	1747	1972
28	Edward Hopper	1882–1967	366	5.2	236	89	41
29	Amedeo Modigliani	1884–1920	242	13.4	6	30	206
30	Joan Miró	1893–1983	2,050	27.7	414	583	1061
31	Salvador Dalí	1904–1989	1,000	13.5	402	306	292
32	Frida Kahlo	1907–1954	152	4.9	45	68	38
33	Francis Bacon	1909–1992	584	9.1	50	349	189
34	Robert Motherwell	1915–1991	1,931	37.9	274	1102	555
35	Jean-Michel Basquiat	1960–1988	600–1,000	66.7	237	147	56

★ ★ ★ SPRING 2023 ★ ★ ★

CITY ARTS & LECTURES

presents

May 4 MICHIO KAKU

May 6 LAURA DERN
& DIANE LADD   *Mother & Daughter* ←

Seriously! → May 9 JOHN WATERS

May 11 ABRAHAM VERGHESE

May 16 TOM HANKS

May 18 JAVIER ZAMORA   *Your favorite
host from Bravo*

May 19 ANDY COHEN ←

Jun 2 BRANDON TAYLOR

*New poetry
collection* Jun 3 STACEY ABRAMS

→ Jun 9 OCEAN VUONG *and more!*

LIVE AT THE SYDNEY GOLDSTEIN THEATER

275 Hayes Street, San Francisco

TICKETS: 415-392-4400 or CITYARTS.NET

DALE DICKEY

[ACTOR]

"WHAT? I'VE BEEN DOING THIS FOR HOW LONG?"

A few of the accessories central to Dale Dickey's role in *A Love Song*:
Sturdy boots
Black hair band
Red bracelet
A necklace with three tiny birds and beads (lost in New Orleans)

O ver the course of four decades, Dale Dickey has appeared in more than 130 supporting roles in TV, on film, and in theaters. A Knoxville, Tennessee, native who began acting at age nine, she has worked alongside Jack Nicholson, Jeff Bridges, Sean Penn, Robert Downey Jr., and Toni Collette, among others. Her characters, always in service to the story, are singular creations. Many of them embody mental toughness and expose survivorship's brittle edges. In the opening of 2016's Hell or High Water, *Dickey's character, Elsie, a bank clerk, reveals a surprising subtext in a string of West Texas bank robberies as a gun is held to her head. Dickey's tight exchanges, layered physicality, and masterful facial expressions give the film a distinctive texture. In part due to her performance, it went on to gross $37,999,675 worldwide, far outpacing its $12 million budget.*

Illustration by Kristian Hammerstad

In 2010's Winter's Bone, *Dickey plays Merab, the matriarchal head of an Ozarks family. Acting alongside Jennifer Lawrence in her breakout role, Dickey delivers a riveting performance, portraying a character who confronts meth use, mental illness, violence, and impoverishment. Debra Granik, the film's director, told* IndieWire *that "during the shooting of* Winter's Bone, *Dickey had a revelation and explained that she didn't perceive her character… as a stone-cold sadist, but that there was another layer to her." This interpretation allowed Dickey to shun the pitfalls of a one-dimensional, dark character. Her instinctive acting gave the story a suspenseful complexity and won her the 2011 Independent Spirit Award for Best Supporting Female.*

Now Dickey is stepping into starring roles for the first time. In the 2022 film A Love Song, *written and directed by Max Walker-Silverman, she plays Faye, a sixtyish woman traveling alone, who bides her time fishing, birding, and stargazing at a rural Colorado campground, while she waits for someone from her past. Through her performance, the film explores themes of independence, wanderlust, aging, and grief. For her portrayal, she was nominated for a Gotham Award and an Independent Spirit Award, alongside actors such as Cate Blanchett and Michelle Williams.*

Dale Dickey is an inspiration, someone who has doggedly pursued a career in a difficult industry. At sixty-one, she is still accomplishing firsts, still channeling resilient characters. She has won seven prestigious film festival awards and has been nominated for many more, but the awards are not especially important to her. As long as she keeps working, she's happy.

—*Yvonne Conza*

I. EARLY DAYS

THE BELIEVER: What has changed for you since you first started acting?

DALE DICKEY: In my early years, I was struggling. Struggling. I couldn't get an agent. I was auditioning, waitressing, doing workshops, and constantly acting in plays—it was always this drive I had. I feel like I've been running my whole life too. Maybe I've been running from something, but really it's been toward something. Yet it was never anything specific. I wanted to work. I thought: I can't do anything else. This is why I'm in New York. Go do it. Do it now.

Now that I've been working more and more, I've relaxed a little bit. When I was finally able to quit my multitude of day jobs and had the beauty of making a living as an actor, it was like, Wow, whoa. The years can still be lean—up and down—though I continue to keep working. Yet there's always that fear of: I'll never work again. [*Laughs*] But as I've gotten older and worked with wonderful people, I have a different appreciation for acting. I still feel the love for my craft that I felt back then, when I was also feeling the panic of struggling and trying to audition to get the next job. Today it's more about enjoying the fact that I probably will get another job, and who will I get to work with now? Since I'm older, I can sit back and watch all the wheels turn and enjoy the collaboration that is making the art.

BLVR: In 1984, what was New York like for you?

DD: I moved up there with some friends from college—two good guy friends and another good girlfriend. The four of us slept in bunk beds in a tiny apartment on Columbus Avenue and 106th Street, which was rough at that time. One day I drove into the city and I turned right on a red light… because you can do that in Tennessee. Well, you can't do that in New York City. [*Laughs*]

The cop had this grin on his face. "Oh, honey," he said, and handed me his card. "Welcome to New York. You might need some help one day. Take this with you." He let me go with a warning. I was not naive, but in many ways I was still quite innocent. I loved my time in New York and worked in so many different restaurants and bars. My eyes were opened to the real world.

BLVR: Surviving New York is not easy.

DD: When I lived on Ninety-Ninth and Broadway, there was a homeless woman at the Ninety-Sixth Street subway stop. She was my age, with long hair like mine, but hers was white. It looked as if she had never stopped crying. Her eyes were this piercing blue, like Meg Foster's, the actress. I was poor and had a shitty apartment, but this woman had nothing. I couldn't get on the subway and not give her my quarter. It makes you feel grateful, no matter how down-and-out you think you are. I just thought, There but for the grace of God. It made me realize how lucky I was that

I had family and friends and I probably would never have to be homeless—someone would put me up on their couch.

I loved my years in New York and learned a lot. I worked my ass off. I've gone back there for work, but it doesn't fit with my love of the outdoors. Part of my time there, I felt trapped. I didn't have the money to get out. Central Park wasn't going to cut it for my nature fix. When I go back now, I love the energy—that energy of New York with people of all different places, colors, and walks of life intermingling. But the canyons that tall buildings create make me feel depressed. I have got to get that sunshine.

BLVR: Looking back at those early years, what advice do you have for actors who are just starting out?

DD: Perseverance. I tell young actors: One of the hardest things that I struggled with when I was younger was comparing my progress to that of friends from college. Asking: Why are they getting those auditions and I can't get an agent? That is an ugly and dark place that eats you alive. Everybody's journey is different, and some people are going to make it overnight. They're going to have a leading role right off the bat, like Jennifer Lawrence in *Winter's Bone*. She had that raw, beautiful talent, and you just knew it. She's also such a great and grounded person. At least she was back then, and I'm sure she still is now. I knew Hollywood wasn't going to change her.

I never thought, When am I going to do a lead role? I just wanted to keep working, and that got me recurring roles that were smaller. I was in and out of everything, but I kept getting jobs. I'd say: just keep working and don't focus on how big the role is, but how your role fits into the story, because every role is as important as the next.

II. A LEAD ROLE

BLVR: The media has proclaimed, thunderously, that you can carry a film. Does that confirmation change anything for you?

DD: That's a complex question. I was very relieved that I didn't mess up Max Walker-Silverman's beautiful vision.

I have spent so much of my time in supporting roles, in the background, that it's almost where I'm more comfortable. There's a huge responsibility that comes with carrying the lead, but I learned a lot and I would love the challenge again.

BLVR: What aspect of making this film [*A Love Song*] was the most satisfying?

DD: Filming in the outdoors. I love nature and related to Faye [her character] a lot. It was also my first job during COVID. Our eleven-member crew masked up and we all felt very safe in the outdoors.

BLVR: How did you develop Faye's internal and external dialogue?

DD: The internal and external dialogue has a lot to do with her not breaking her routine. Max talked a lot about that being what she's surviving on—her daily routine. Everything's very deliberate with Faye, and very different from the way I am. As you can tell, I'm very animated. Max worked a lot with me. I think he had studied acting. He was terrific with getting me back into that space.

BLVR: I'm curious about that necklace you wore and how that spoke to your character. You also wore a wedding band and had a red string and black rubber bracelet on your left wrist. How did those things help develop Faye's character?

DD: I am the kind of actress—maybe it's coming from theater—where wardrobe always informs how I feel about the character. I tried on a couple of different pairs of shoes, and one felt too manly. I went with a pair that had grace and a little bit of femininity to the boot. It gave me a sturdiness that I needed.

We also had a wonderful costume designer, Stine Dahlman. She was very specific about what Faye wore. The shoes, jewelry, and clothes were precisely chosen styles and colors. My hair was as is and I wore no makeup. I just put on sunscreen, covered up

Clockwise from upper left: Wes Studi (left) and Dale Dickey (right) in A Love Song; *Dale Dickey in* A Love Song; *Dale Dickey, Marty Grace Dennis, Scout Engbring, Gregory Hope, Jesse Hope, and Sam Engbring in* A Love Song; *Wes Studi in* A Love Song. *Photos courtesy of Bleecker Street Media.*

some zits, and went on set. That black band was for pulling my hair back.

BLVR: Oh, that was a hair band.

DD: Yes, the black one was a hair band, because whenever you see Faye working on something, she pulls her hair up. The red band was actually a special memento that Stine's friend had made, and she wanted to use it as a tribute to her friend who she felt was like Faye. Stine chose the necklaces as well. I had a tiny, beautiful one with three tiny birds and beads, almost a choker. Unfortunately, I lost that necklace in New Orleans on a job. It just fell off my neck and I thought, Well, shit, but you have to let that go. The other necklace I still have and I keep it in a box. It belonged to Max's mother, Lindsey. Stine wanted just a little bit of color and something that represented the land. That necklace had this little picture of the Telluride valley that a local artist does the prints for. The jewelry was very specific and informed who Faye was—very down-to-earth.

BLVR: Faye is very self-reliant. I wonder if you could talk about self-reliance as a strength and a weakness.

DD: Good question. I think about being self-reliant a lot. I've been so busy the past couple of years—traveling and away for extended periods of time for various films. Steve, my husband, couldn't go with me, because of the COVID restrictions. He was here at home, dealing with all my paperwork coming in. I've always been the one that did all my paperwork and accounting, but it became overwhelming. I needed his help. Yet I don't want to rely on him and depend on him, because what if he's not here?

When I was growing up, my mom was a Faye. There's a lot of my mother and my sister in Faye. In her early thirties, my mom was divorced with three difficult children. She went back to work. She fixed our car. When she'd take us skiing, she knew how to put the gas in the damn carburetor and how to change a tire. She would go into the garage and fix the plumbing by wrapping it with tape, something her friends taught her. She learned how to do all those things because she had no choice. She had to do it on her own. It's very important to be self-reliant, but it's also dangerous to not ask for help. And that's why I finally said to my husband, "I need some help with keeping up with my accounting. There's too much going on."

I love Amy Sedaris, and there's a wonderful image from one of her shows where a guy goes, "I just wish I knew what was going on in that head of yours." Then they show this old black-and-white image of these monkeys in a duck pond and there's just chaos—so I said, "Steve, I have monkeys and ducks going on." Not asking for help can put you in a dark place. There's knowing when it's time to ask for help, and then there's knowing when you need to do it on your own, because, if you're by yourself, you've got to learn how to do it to survive.

III. "I TAKE THE JOBS"

BLVR: You've now worked with two great independent filmmakers: Debra Granik on *Winter's Bone*, and now Max. How important is it for you to choose to work with those people, instead of taking the parts that pay the most money?

DD: That's a great question. I was asked that recently and responded, "Well, I don't have the luxury of turning down work." I didn't mean that in a snarky way. My career has been built on: you take the next job. I need my health insurance. Steadily, over the years, I've made a little bit more money here and there, but I've never been a series regular. That's a whole different level of money. I take the jobs. Recently, I've turned down roles because I can be a little choosier now. My agent said, "It's OK to say no. You don't have to do everything. You want to do everything, but you can't." So I am a little choosier at this time. But I have to tell you that I feel spoiled, having worked with Max, and I want to hold on to that beautiful feeling we all had working together. I felt that way after *Winter's Bone* too.

BLVR: I feel like *A Love Song* counters the caricature of "cowboy-ism" and Westerns. It understands that women from those parts have complex, intersecting stories. It seemed to me that Max is sort of saying, *Here's a side to the story that's been overlooked.*

DD: Yes, it's true. Debra does the same thing—wanting to show people who have been marginalized, or who have had their distinctive stories shown only in stereotypical ways. One of my favorite characters in *A Love Song* is the postman. I don't remember there being a postman in the first draft. When I read the next draft and the postman was there, I thought, Ah, perfect: a friendly, quirky courier dispatching correspondence—that's what keeps Faye going. This coincided with the time that the orange idiot who used to be at the White House and the postmaster general Louis DeJoy tried to dismantle the post office. I was like, "You see how important mail is?" My father is ninety-five and he still uses an old typewriter. He doesn't have a cell phone, a computer, or a TV. He tells me, "I'm sorry, honey. I know that's what you do, but I don't like TV and film." However, he lives for his letters, and now all his friends are dying, and so he lives for his mail and his newspapers, and that connection is important. I know young kids think, Why don't you just pick up your cell phone or get on the internet? But there's a beauty in that written mail.

BLVR: What did Max and you most want to convey regarding Faye's story arc?

DD: The fact that she is a survivor and took a leap of faith. It didn't work out the way she had hoped, but it was what she needed to do to be able to move on with her life. By the end, there is a rebirth by climbing to the top of that mountain and seeing the stars for the first time and letting go of other things. It was also about moving on from loneliness, learning to live life alone while embracing hope and the importance of connecting with people.

Particularly because of COVID, I think people will relate to this film on many levels, especially the isolation and loneliness and wanting to connect with people. I remember feeling lucky that I had my husband during COVID, even though we wanted to kill each other sometimes. But I had so many friends that were completely by themselves, so we would do these masked-up, six-feet-apart walks together to give them some sort of connection.

BLVR: It's interesting you mentioned COVID. In an early scene the film shows the calendar with June 2020 followed by Faye marking September 17 as the date she'll leave the campgrounds. The year 2020 is a COVID time stamp. So the film kind of talks about COVID without talking about it. That calendar also had bush plane images for every month.

DD: The bush planes. Yes, very definitely—those related to a whole slew of other weird jobs that Faye had. She had worked as a deep-sea diver with wrecks off the coast of South America and built trucks with her dad. Those details were in tiny scenes that ended up being cut because they weren't needed. But with the calendar scene, Max said, "Close your eyes and whatever date you hit, that's it." But you're right. COVID was part of the story. Max doesn't miss any details. Boy, is that kid smart.

IV. FROM THE HEART

BLVR: In your own life, what books are you drawn to?

DD: I have to admit I was never a good reader, and it's something that I am working on. I love poetry and reading short stories. I just bought Brian Cox's biography because I love him as an actor and studied with him. He was my teacher years ago when I studied in England for the summer. I'm very curious to read it. I wish I could list a ton of intellectual books that I've read, but I haven't.

BLVR: But you're reading a lot of scripts, and when you're breaking down the scripts, it seems like you're doing something special.

DD: I am. I've done a lot of films that have been adapted from books, and I always read the book, even if it's completely different from the way the script has come out. I love doing research on scripts and reading history books when I'm working on period pieces. I did a film in Ireland two years ago where we jumped back and forth from the 1500s to the present, and I did a tremendous amount of research on Irish history.

With this script, I felt I was trying to find what would be in between those lines, all the subtext in my own mind. Wes Studi, who plays Lito, and I made the decision not to talk too much about the characters. We wanted our interactions to be spontaneous. We both had knowledge about Faye and Lito and had talked some about what they had shared. What they have in common now was what they shared back then.

BLVR: In 2015, you gave a commencement speech at the University of Tennessee, and you said: "No matter where you end up on your quest, whether it's a big city or a small town, your story is unique and important. Remember what has shaped you." Can you elaborate on this?

DD: Well, I'm surprised you saw that commencement speech. I can't watch it [tears up]. When I was asked to do that, it was a really difficult time in my life. My mother was dying of Alzheimer's and—

MICROINTERVIEW WITH WO CHAN, PART VI

THE BELIEVER: I admire the urgency—and, is it anger?—in some of these poems. In the second-person prose poems, as you read down the lines, it's like watching a fuse burn toward a bomb.

WO CHAN: Yes, there is anger. I think about how I can catalog and throw everything about my body at the state, and it does not matter, because to the state I will always be a number, an alien number. Still, there are memories that I protect. That I don't write about. I always thought I was supposed to write about my deportation hearing, for instance, but I never could bring myself to do it. I actually don't know if I want to share that moment of my life with the whole world.

BLVR: I remember you alluding to that on Facebook. In *Togetherness*, you do include some of the letters of support that you gathered during the deportation appeal. Why did you decide to include them?

WC: There are multiple purposes, one of which is to ground the reader in my real-world experience. But I'm also fascinated by the linguistic performance of the letters. There's a certain algebra or calculation that goes into these kinds of letters of appeal. Each person writes toward a particular idea of what makes a good American citizen. My friend's dad, the city manager, wrote, "The Chans always paid their taxes on time and they're always the last ones to get home, to go home." *That's* why we should stay in America? It's just wild. ★

BLVR: I'm sorry.

DD: No, it's OK. It was just a lot of pressure. I wasn't sure I could do it. I was like—I don't know how to do this. I was listening to all these other commencement speeches, trying to make sure I said the perfect things. They told me: "Dale, just speak from your heart," and that's what I did.

BLVR: The speech seemed to share a synchronicity with many of the themes in *A Love Song*.

DD: I think maybe it's my whole life that led me to this role. I grew up near the Great Smoky Mountains and we were lucky that my parents, despite being divorced when I was very little, both took us to the mountains. We got to go to the beach and be outdoors. In California, my husband and I do a tremendous amount of camping. It's our saving grace of living in a tiny LA apartment. We've really enjoyed the beauty of the state.

I am very much like Faye in many ways—comfortable in nature. I crave it. It's where I feel the most spiritual. It's nice to have someone to share it with. You do need your alone time for meditation, but that's one of the questions in the movie: What is love if you don't have someone to share it with? We all face that.

V. "THE MOST WRINKLED PERSON IN HOLLYWOOD"

BLVR: Tell me about how you got that role in *The Pledge* [2001].

DD: This is what really happened. I get this audition call from Don Phillips who did all of Sean Penn's movies. I go into Don's office and I'm waiting to read the script. We're just talking and he goes, "Dale, I don't need you to read. I can look at your resume and tell you can act. I can look at you physically and tell you're right for this role. I'll bring you back in a few days to read for Sean personally. You want to know the reason you're here?" And I went, "Yes, please." [*Laughs*] This after he went into saying we never see new people— meaning outside their agency. He goes, "I looked at your resume and way down here at the bottom it said the University of Tennessee." He had been on a basketball scholarship at UT in the '60s and he wanted to meet a fellow Volunteer.

He wasn't from Tennessee, but he had gone there. That is the sole reason I ended up in that room.

BLVR: You've worked with so many great actors over the years. How have they shaped your career?

DD: I've had so many people who've been influential in my life, but I do have to go back to Sean Penn. That was an audition that came out of the blue. Anyway, I just lucked out, so lucked out. Being on that set in a supporting role like that was the first time I'd been on a film where I was there all the time, even though I was in the background. I watched everything and Sean kept pulling me over. "Come on, look behind the camera." He taught me how to watch dailies. The fact that I kept getting positive feedback—and I was working—gave me the strength to continue. That film was a huge turning point for me.

I didn't see Sean or hear from him for eighteen years, since obviously we don't run in the same circles. Then out of the blue, my agent says, "Sean Penn wants to talk to you." I'm like, "What?" He called me about doing this new film, *Flag Day* [2021], starring his daughter, Dylan, who's a tremendous actress. I met Dylan and Hopper—Sean's son— when they were kids on *The Pledge*. They were tiny and now they're adults. Sean said to me, "Dale, I want you to play this really small role, but it's important." He goes, "You're too young to be a grandma. We're going to have to age you up." I said, "Sean, you haven't seen me in eighteen years— you do know I am the most wrinkled person in Hollywood, except for Nick Nolte. You ain't going to do any aging up." That Sean kept me in mind after I worked with him, and Debra Granik hired me again [*Leave No Trace*, 2018]—I've been really blessed.

BLVR: Reflecting on your career, what does a snapshot in your head of the various roles you've done look like?

DD: There are many roles in films I did that haven't even seen the light of day. I've done so many small indie and short films by young directors and writers. I told my agent, "If it's a good script, I want to do it." It's surreal how time has passed so quickly and all of a sudden I'm sixty years old. Part of me feels like, What? I've been doing this for how long? I started doing theater when I was nine. I was supposed to be going to school but I was in play rehearsals. I was always late to class and never did my homework, but my teachers knew I was doing something creative. I was reading—reading Shakespeare. I always knew that I just had to keep acting. It was like—how do they say—God or whatever gives you a gift, and you just have to keep chiseling away and mining that gift.

BLVR: How was it dealing with the different aspects of the business—the job of working with agents and industry people?

DD: Oh, they're often at odds with each other. I've never been a good businessperson. A lot of the training conservatories for actors now, and even then when I was in school taught the business end. At the University of Tennessee, they had a LORT [League of Resident Theatres] company in residence at the Clarence Brown Theatre and they brought in professional actors from New York who showed us how to do a resume and go to open calls. But the business end has always frightened me. People used to ask me back then, "Why don't you have a manager and a publicist?" or this and that, and I'd say, "Well, I don't because I can't even get an agent."

BLVR: I read that when you started out, you were without representation for twelve years.

DD: I was always on my own. When I finally did have agents during my career, they either died or retired. In 2007, during the writers' strike, I found a beautiful home with an agency—one that I had tried for years to get into. I'm still with that agency and I adore them. They are wonderful people and good businesspeople. David Shaul advises me well without pushing me. Maybe I'd be further along in my career if I had a publicist and a manager. I don't know. It wasn't my path. I just wanted to work but wasn't making the kind of money where I could pay all those other people.

I do worry that oftentimes the production and the money side of the business overtake the artistic vision. That's why I like small indie films so much. They are focused on the story. Not that the big productions aren't, but there's so much more money involved. To go from a huge set into the tiny but impactful world of *A Love Song*—I love that. It's the pure, simple art of telling the story.

BLVR: I went back and watched a lot of your movies. You are one of those actors that audiences gravitate to. How is it that you are a magnet for the eyes?

DD: [*Laughs*] That's a beautiful thing to say. I've never thought of myself that way. People ask, "Well, how many takes did the scene take?" I have no idea. I don't pay attention. For me, it's about getting on set and doing my work. I'm paying attention to my character and to the story.

BLVR: If you had the opportunity to go back and talk to nine-year-old Diana Dale Dickey, what would you say to her?

DD: *This is what you're supposed to be doing. Just keep going. Somebody put you here for a reason. Keep doing it and love it.* My work has taken me very far away from home, but I wouldn't have done anything differently. I recently had that discussion with my father when I was in Tennessee. My dad's still alive, but how much of my mother's life did I miss? She was my sole supporter and was nothing but positive. She kept telling me, "Look, if this is what you want to do, you're going to do it." There was no pushing or judgment.

I was the kid who leaves home and pursues a career. But as I've gotten older, I've asked myself, Shouldn't I have just stayed home and enjoyed all the time with my family? But there are those of us who are meant to live a different life—to go out and explore the world. It's very important to me now to cherish my time with my family and friends—and to stop and smell those roses. They're not there forever.

BLVR: That's true. When they announced your name at the 2011 Independent Spirit Awards, you closed your eyes tightly for several seconds. What did that moment mean to you?

DD: It was like I was out of my body. It was such a new and different experience for me. I was so nervous and I felt so honored to be there with my fellow actors and all these brilliant people around me. I was extra nervous because the award was the first one to be announced. The producers told us not to thank them and to "speak from your heart." But I remember very little about it. I remember trying to shut my eyes and sitting there expecting someone else to walk onto the stage. It was a good feeling. Then they called my name and I had to go up there. ★

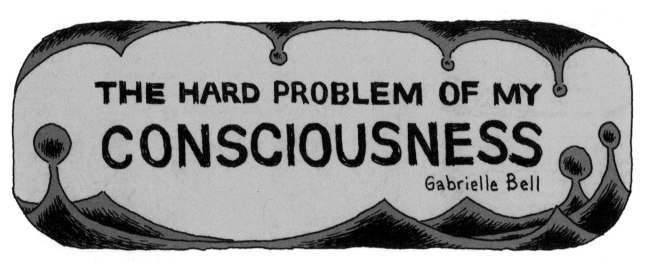

THE HARD PROBLEM OF MY CONSCIOUSNESS

Gabrielle Bell

Halfway through November already? Halfway through my life already? (Assuming I'll live to be 92).

The first half wasn't as satisfying as I'd hoped, TBH (of my life and the of month).

I try not to think about it that way. Time's not linear! Time doesn't exist!

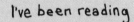

In spite of thinking that, time flies by.

WAIT!

THE BUS OF LIFE

I've been reading

JULIAN JAYNES

THE ORIGIN OF CONSCIOUSNESS IN THE BREAK-DOWN OF THE BICAMERAL MIND.

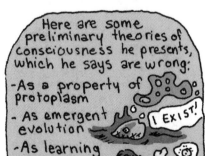

Here are some preliminary theories of consciousness he presents, which he says are wrong:

- As a property of protoplasm
- As emergent evolution
- As learning
- As "helpless spectator"
- As a property of matter (???)

I EXIST!

HELP, I'VE GOT NO FREE WILL!

There's been a bunch more theories since this book was published, such as "the stoned ape theory."

The one most convincing to me, which the writer is most dismissive of, is the metaphysical theory.

I ENDOW YOU WITH CONSCIOUSNESS.

Meanwhile, I'm struggling with the problem of my own consciousness.

VOUS VOULEZ... OUAIS OUAIS

For example, right now, it's being hijacked by the voice of this French man eating and drinking on his Zoom meeting.

TOUT DE SUITE SLRRP

My problem with consciousness is that I have trouble pointing it at something. When I meditate, I've got all sorts of fascinating thoughts. When I sit down to write, my thoughts are boring.

His voice is beautiful, soft, and gentle, and yet so annoying.

HE MUST BE VERY GOOD-LOOKING. HE SOUNDS LIKE HE HAS NO IDEA WHAT REJECTION FEELS LIKE.

Earlier, on the subway, I remembered an exercise Emmanuel Carrère discussed in his book Yoga.

You stand without holding the pole, and you keep your balance by moving with the car. It should bring the mind and body into the moment.

I got to thinking about that book.

HE'S ALSO DEALING WITH CONSCIOUSNESS...

AND HE DROVE HIMSELF INSANE TRYING TO UNDERSTAND IT.

HOW DOES ONE WRITE A BOOK LIKE THAT, ANYWAY?

ASIDE FROM COMPOSING CLEAR, ELEGANT SENTENCES, THE AUTHOR MUST IMPLY THAT THEY HAVE SOME SPECIAL KNOWLEDGE THAT THE READER NEEDS TO KNOW...

IT DOESN'T EVEN MATTER IF THEY DON'T HAVE—

WHAT THE—

I suddenly had the feeling that I was literally insane. All my thoughts, though seemingly coherent, were just a string of haphazard, undeveloped, untested notions, meaning nothing.

WHAT DO I EVEN MEAN BY "AUTHORIAL TONE"??

HOW AM I EVEN ALIVE?

A REVIEW OF

USERS

BY COLIN WINNETTE

In Colin Winnette's new novel, *Users*, virtual reality has reached its final stages of perfection. An unnamed corporation, having invented what it calls Original Experiences, helps users render their inner visions in HD and act out fantasies of lethal detail and precision. These Original Experiences never have to dictate the substance, the dream stuff, of customers: the less specific the software, the richer the users' experience. In response to the light touch of its products, the corporation receives a "flood of creativity" from users.

Winnette's protagonist, Miles, is one of the corporation's top employees, and both the best and the worst possible person to be in charge of others' speculative reveries. Capable of intimacy only on his own terms, Miles is obsessed with and scared of other people. He fears his responsibility to his loved ones, because he cannot contend with the standard results of such social ties: occasional disappointment, interpersonal gaffes. Every interaction Miles has with his wife, Claire, is thus approached as if on the emotional terrain of a chessboard. "If he was careful, he could fix this," he thinks tactically at some point, in the midst of a conversation. "He had to choose his next move wisely." Rarely able to stay convinced of the righteousness of his self-assertions, Miles lashes out at others, then minces away. By the end of the book, the most he can say of his older daughter is that she is "a person he'd spent time with."

When users come close to discovering violations of the company's privacy policy, Miles is tapped to manage a burgeoning PR crisis. His solution is a grand distraction in the form of the Egg: a glorified piece of smart furniture that allows people to pilot virtual reality scenes as full-body experiences. The catch is that the experiences are shared—manipulated and negotiated by other people in other Eggs. Users jockey with one another "to protect their preferred experiences"; in this push and pull, they are meant to eventually agree "upon the terms of a given reality," and finally live in "chaotic harmony."

Tech companies love to circuitously reinvent that which already exists. In the same way that Uber repackaged the taxi and DoorDash the pizza delivery, Miles comes up with the millennia-old concept of politics. People settling their realities via degrees of persuasion and aggression, cosigning agendas in the hopes of seeing them persist: this is what happens in any kind of political community. It is also what happens, on a micro scale, in a romantic relationship. Miles is bad at being part of either, and when he enters the Egg, it is only to be alone. He goes in seeking literally "nothing," hoping to be released from his impact on other people and the risk of "mak[ing] it worse."

Despite his company's penchant for data harvesting, Miles's personality is thus not so much extractive as entropic; he thrashes about, voiding himself of energy and feeling, and in the process becomes impenetrable to others. When he does communicate, it is only to pass on what obsesses him to someone else; Miles sees intimacy as a means of unburdening himself. His worries are like a sickness that he can get over only by giving them to another person. Men like Miles run from the prospect of fucking up, from the disapproval of loved ones, and their flight is always into the rounded fantasy of the zero. To be nothing is to be unusable, unaccountable. A notion like this may seem objectionable to readers, until we remember that we, too, nurse it. To never feel the thwang of interpersonal tension, to live in a self that is slack and spent and upon which no demands can be made—for these reasons and others, we turn to contemporary tech. Our algorithms and feeds become more personalized, and the distance between ourselves and others widens.

—*Zoë Hu*

Publisher: *Soft Skull Press* Page count: *288* Price: *$27* Key quote: *"It was a living fantasy, limited only by the speed of your internet and the company's servers."* Shelve next to: *William Gibson, Don DeLillo, Sinclair Lewis* Unscientifically calculated reading time: *One long, relentless doomscroll*

Illustration by Pete Gamlen

A REVIEW OF

PICTURE BOOKS
(IMPRINT)

BY OTTESSA MOSHFEGH, PERCIVAL EVERETT, SAM LIPSYTE, AND LYDIA MILLET

In 2021, Gagosian Publishing, an arm of the influential Gagosian galleries, launched an imprint called Picture Books, conceived by writer Emma Cline with designer Peter Mendelsund, in order to publish fiction by "leading authors," accompanied by work from "celebrated contemporary artists." The hardcover books, beautifully produced, share a trim size and a minimalist, series look. Each has a pocket on its inside front cover, and in each pocket waits a folded poster of the visual work.

As a set, they feel eminently collectible. The first two titles in the series, from 2021, pair Ottessa Moshfegh's story "My New Novel" with *the down payment*, an oil-on-linen piece by painter and musician Issy Wood; and Percival Everett's novella-length "Grand Canyon, Inc." with *Untitled (Original Cowboy)*, a photograph by artist Richard Prince. Gagosian states that the project will give an artist "carte blanche to create an image that is in conversation with the writer's story," which makes it sound as though the point is to explore the possibilities of reverse ekphrasis (when an artist responds to a text with new visual work), though this doesn't entirely bear out. While Wood's painting was created in response to Moshfegh's text, Prince's piece is from the artist's 2013 *Original Cowboy* series. It's a large-scale photograph of sandstone buttes on the Utah–Arizona border. Everett's story, meanwhile, follows a man who grows up in Iowa obsessed with guns, gets rich leading big-game hunts in Kenya for assorted international assholes, then returns to the United States and buys the Grand Canyon. As Gagosian's website argues, both Everett and Prince are "tricksters" known for playing with mythologies of the American West, so it seems what's been paired are two careers; the pairing feels conceptual. The Moshfegh-Wood combo, on the other hand, feels more like a conversation between one specific image and one specific text. Wood's piece works as a kind of grotesque psychological mirror for Moshfegh's story about a failed writer living in LA. A sign that the pairing works: the text kept sending me back to the image, and the image kept returning me to the text. Both Moshfegh's and Everett's stories center loathsome and/or pathetic white American men, and so does Sam Lipsyte's novella-length "Friend of the Pod"—the 2022 addition to the series. Lipsyte's story gives us a middle-aged Gen X-er living in New York City who goes to work for an obnoxious boomer in New Jersey who wants to start a podcast, and the whole thing ends violently when two more awful guys show up. Lipsyte's work is paired with *Untitled*, a digital image by Jordan Wolfson, whose VR piece at the 2017 Whitney Biennial, *Real Violence*, let viewers watch him beat up another man. Here again the pairing feels more conceptual than specific. In an interview Wolfson talks about "selecting" the image—what does that mean? Why does it matter? I suppose some intractable part of my brain got stuck on that word *create* in the original project announcement. One reason acts of reverse ekphrasis might be more interesting than conceptual pairings is because the latter are not uncommon; we see them when a painting appears on the cover of a novel, or a photograph accompanies an online publication of a story.

But seeing an artist provoked by a text, and seeing whatever new thing they make in response sitting next to the text that inspired it—that seems quite special. The most recent addition to the series is Lydia Millet's delightfully odd "Lyrebird," in which a woman gets an invitation to sing, though she's not a singer, at a mysterious man's estate/menagerie; it's paired with an equally delightful acrylic painting, *Eternal Garden*, by Irish artist Genieve Figgis. Further books have been announced, with fiction by Joy Williams, Mary Gaitskill, and Elif Batuman. Whatever the nature of each pairing, all the writers and artists involved do compelling work, so it will be exciting to see which artists Cline assigns to the next batch of writers, and what sort of collaborative energy results.

—*Danielle Dutton*

> **Publisher:** *Gagosian* **Number of books as of winter 2023:** *4* **Price of full collection:** *$150* **Art subjects featured:** *Sandstone buttes, a strange bird in a colorful courtyard, and unhappy people*

119

Illustration by Pete Gamlen

IN VITRO: ON LONGING AND TRANSFORMATION

BY ISABEL ZAPATA

"**M**y psychoanalyst begins our session by saying that the desire to be a mother isn't the same as the desire to have a child." When I read this line, in a book-length essay by Mexican poet Isabel Zapata, I hear the echo of another line with an acutely similar shape: "The desire to die is not the desire to be dead. Anyone who has ever been in love knows this," says Jericho Brown, in a recording of a lecture I listened to some months ago. Is it fair for my mind to link these lines? One concerns the desire to make life; the other, the desire for life to end. Maybe they speak, if from opposite directions, into one shared void: the space between condition and action, name and object, thought and touch, estar y ser, living and life—the space where so many of our griefs begin.

Reading Isabel Zapata's sparks of thought, collected throughout the author's process of in vitro fertilization, I am brought to the edge of many voids. Her fragmented prose chronicles the experience of becoming pregnant, of giving birth, of early motherhood. We are witness to the misogynistic horrors of the medical-industrial complex and to the gendered cultural imaginations of motherhood. The book recounts not only the anticipated birth of Zapata's child but also the death of her mother. Though her work appears, in moments, to be a remembrance of the past, it could also be regarded, in other moments, as an act of dismemberment: hopes, beliefs, desires, and expectations come apart in Zapata's spiraling lines. We are given a telling of daughterhood and motherhood that doesn't shy away from the jagged, the unfathomable. We are never spared the difficulty of the body or of the mind.

Some English-language readers may be reminded of Maggie Nelson's fragmentary style when reading Zapata's work, though Nelson herself reminds us that "fragments are as old as the hills, which are fragments of mountains." Paragraphs sit like islands in white space, occasionally accompanied by watercolor renditions of ultrasounds, or by medical charts. "No ancient civilization could resist the allure of using imaginary lines to connect the little shining dots that appeared in the night sky," Zapata reminds us at one juncture in her prose. She must have known that her readers, too, could not resist the pull to imagine the lines between her shining paragraphs, to cohere the incoherent, to sew her book together. Zapata anticipates the parallel task of cohering the world for her baby, making it intelligible, "showing her how sunlight hits certain objects, shining until it hurts them." This is a question Zapata's work confronts with a steady gaze: What are the risks of true illumination? A sun, which illuminates, must also burn.

Like Nelson, Zapata braids quotations throughout her writing; a reader swims out again and again from the shores of others' thinking. In this way, the book seems only to accrete meaning, never arriving at any single mode of thought, resisting our desire for culmination. The poet Jorie Graham reminds us that a poem might "stop" instead of "end." I think, by necessity and to its great credit, this is a book that stops. Instead of tying the text neatly together, lulling us with the promise of completion, Zapata permits her book to fray.

"Words are alive… the entire world is contained inside them," writes Zapata in one moment of the book. But the book itself seems bruised by all that cannot be named. Zapata is a writer who speaks via her silences, who signals toward the void. Of course, the entire world is not contained inside words; of course, there is a grammar to our silence. Anyone who has ever been in love knows this.

—*Ricardo Frasso Jaramillo*

Publisher: *Coffee House Press* Page count: *160* Price: *$16.95* Key quote: "*We already have hopes and beliefs about you, and we deposit them into your ghost before you exist, not even knowing you will exist.*" Shelve next to: *Josefina Vicens, Alejandra Pizarnik, Clarice Lispector, Valeria Luiselli* Unscientifically calculated reading time: *One characteristically turbulent flight between Bogotá and JFK*

Illustration by Pete Gamlen

COVER TO COVER

SURVEYING THE COVERS OF GREAT BOOKS, AS THEY CHANGE ACROSS TIME AND COUNTRY.
IN THIS ISSUE: *GIOVANNI'S ROOM* BY JAMES BALDWIN

compiled by Eliza Browning

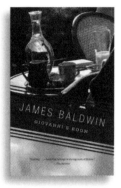

UNITED STATES
Vintage,
2013

UNITED STATES
Ace Books,
1959

PORTUGAL
Companhia das Letras,
2018

POLAND
Państwowy Instytut
Wydawniczy, 1991

UNITED STATES
Dial Press, 1956
(first edition)

UNITED KINGDOM
Everyman's Library,
2016

THAILAND
Library House,
2020

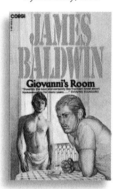

UNITED KINGDOM
Corgi Books,
1977

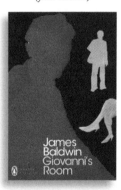

UNITED KINGDOM
Penguin Modern
Classics, 2001

DENMARK
Gyldendal,
2019

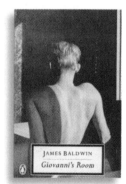

UNITED STATES
Penguin,
1990

UNITED KINGDOM
Penguin Modern
Classics, 2007

WHAT WERE YOU WAITING FOR

A NEW POEM

by Aria Aber

It was a spectacular spring: sparrows bickering in the trees, the street carts
smelling of syrupy cashews in front of the Jewish Museum—
you bought flowers, said *Hi* to the Afghan guards, got a croissant and a café au lait.
At first, every day seemed like someone else's dream:
you were there, you said, because you were writing a novel,
but mainly you were drinking the overly sweet, gratis prosecco at the Nationalgalerie.
You felt something like love for Kirchner's *Potsdamer Platz*, the prostitute's hat.
How is the research going? Have you read the new Rooney?
You wore silver heels to the new Odeon and cried during the Iranian movie
when the actress eats a salted pomegranate in the dark.
Kombucha in the park, picking blue flowers, and watching your friends
watch the handsome clouds pass through the sky.
It was horrible what was going on back home, wasn't it? It was just like *Andorra*.
A tear ran down your cheek and into the grass.
I want you to behave like a girl with no father, said one of your lovers.
You rode the bus back to Friedrichshain at 5 a.m. with your dress torn under your coat,
a dogged joy in your heart. You were writing a novel, you said,
but you just read your horoscope and watched *Schitt's Creek* on repeat most of the time.
You were nannying for a family in Mitte, and one in Prenzlauer Berg.
Two springs passed like that, not writing a thing. Then you were sitting
on your stoop, the shorts damp and sticking to your thighs. There was the scent
of garbage and apples and impending rain, voices of children rose
from the neighboring yards: soon the sparrows would start bickering again.
Any day now, the astrology app said, your new life was about to begin.

PLACE

THE ATLANTA HOTEL, BANGKOK, THAILAND

by Leslie Carol Roberts

FEATURES:

* ✶ Spartan rooms
* ✶ A writerly legacy
* ✶ A military legacy
* ✶ Cold pineapple juice

When it opened its doors for the first time some seventy years ago, the Atlanta Hotel was the first hostelry in Bangkok with a swimming pool. It might also have been the first to later ban sex tourists: a quietly aggressive sign by the front door, placed there in 2002, states: SEX TOURISTS NOT WELCOME.

In the 1960s and '70s, the hotel was a gathering place for writers and artists. It was also popular with US military brass and others passing through as part of the war effort. It was during these years that Bangkok's well-known sex trade exploded, and the Atlanta seemed destined to be sucked permanently into that culture.

The Atlanta is the legacy of the Henn family—the father, Max Henn, fled Nazi Germany, and in 1952 he wound up in Thailand, where he started a pharmaceutical lab that sold cobra venom to the United States. He fell in love with a Thai chemist who worked in the lab, Mukda Buresbamrungkarn, and they married and had a son, Charles Henn. But the venom lab did not thrive, so to make ends meet, Max converted rooms at the lab's offices into accommodations. He was, apparently, a reluctant hotelier.

When the Henns divorced, the hotel was left to Mukda's family to manage. It fell into disrepair, but the Henns retained ownership. The Atlanta devolved over the years into a seedy joint that catered to those frequenting the nearby notorious red-light districts along Sukhumvit Road, Soi Cowboy, and Nana Plaza, go-go bars packed with young Thai women and men, many dressed in costumes, naughty schoolchildren, and so on.

But the story took a surprising turn. In the late 1980s, the Atlanta was re-embraced by Charles, who had been sent away to Oxford and Cambridge for school when his parents divorced. Max and Mukda had then pursued their own lives and careers away from the hotel and Thailand. The revived Atlanta was once again popular among writers and artists such as Elizabeth Gilbert, who stayed there on her *Eat, Pray, Love* tour. And unlike other "writers' hotels" such as the Ritz in Paris, this was one that a writer could actually afford.

When I visited, in October 2022, the hotel was emerging from Thailand's COVID pandemic restrictions. Its "soft opening" was geared toward returning guests and friends of returning guests (I had stayed there in the early 2000s and had also lived in Bangkok as a journalist for two stints). As I arrived, a liveried doorman greeted this traveler, swinging open the wood-framed glass doors to reveal the original, largely untouched art deco lobby.

This is the Atlanta. In the cotton-candy-pink and red-vinyl mid-century café, a Dutch family and scattered solo travelers tuck into an array of Thai dishes and Thai coffees, alongside eggs and toast and cappuccinos. A cold glass of fresh pineapple juice arrives at reception on a small silver tray, and I am told by the cheerful desk clerks to "not rush. Sit, please," as they carry the tray to a soft sofa. The staff is just as gracious and kind as I recalled. The floors gleam. The stacks of ATLANTA notepaper and pencils are ready for me to jot down thoughts. In addition to a cozy writers' nook with rolltop desks, the lobby offers a sixteen-page booklet that provides advice on haggling, hailing taxis, cleanliness, and appropriate attire for visiting Buddhist shrines.

The rooms and suites remain Spartan, with all the trappings of a solid budget hotel, from the scratchy towels to the tiny packets of dandruff shampoo. But each has been freshly painted and new drapes have been hung. The vinyl floors are impeccable and the tiled bathrooms spotless. And there is still the pool. Across the open-air lobby, the gardens give way to the large swimming pool and smaller ponds, where the resident tortoise community lounges in the shade. Toward the end of a day, after taking in wats and shops in Bangkok, I can be found here. ✶

Illustration by Eden Weingart

THE PUZZLE OF INCREDIBLY WIDE AND DEEP KNOWLEDGE

IF YOU COMPLETE THIS PUZZLE, YOU ARE A GENERALIST OF BROAD SKILL AND GREAT RENOWN

by Wyna Liu; edited by Benjamin Tausig

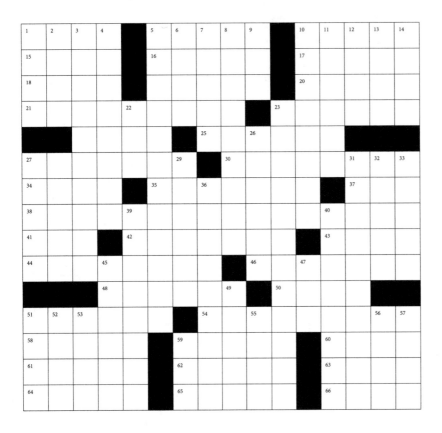

ACROSS

1. "Safe from ___" (1991 Massive Attack single)
5. Concord, for one
10. Monastery VIP
15. Vrksasana (___ pose)
16. Tax-free savings plans named for a Delaware senator who disliked taxes
17. Like marzipan pigs, in Germany
18. Weymouth of Tom Tom Club
19. "To God," literally
20. Really fancy
21. Cheeseburger's cousin
23. Dog-like animals that are in fact more closely related to cats
24. Recipient of fundraising calls, perhaps
25. Way of being loved or smashed
27. Place to stare into space in southern California?
30. Women in a crude British subculture of the late '90s to early 2000s
34. ___ fresca (colorful refreshment)
35. What some points can be exchanged for
37. Latin 101 word
38. Modern digital proof of ownership
41. Fastest expansion team to win a World Series in MLB history, on the scoreboard (2001)
42. Brings around to, as an idea
43. Station above which MSG was constructed in the 1960s
44. Had weight
46. Nat King Cole played him in "St. Louis Blues"
48. Contributes
50. Feels crummy
51. Cover material?
54. Genre for Candlemas and Saint Vitus
58. Largo, essentially
59. Context for an ace
60. Fish whose Chinese name translates to "dragon tongue"
61. Pritzker-winning architect Ando
62. Mountain range neighboring Tian Shan and Hindu Kush
63. Added to the chain, briefly
64. Cutlery that is the form of a "Toy Story 4" character
65. Grilled and sliced
66. Just manages, with "out"

DOWN

1. Letters in a bar
2. Piece that's the basis for "The Goldberg Variations"
3. Let it out!
4. Homestyle dish described in the fifth-century Roman recipe collection "Apicius"
5. They can be annoyingly case-sensitive
6. Cabbed it, say
7. Not on the level
8. Negative spaces?
9. Curvy shape
10. Check for bugs
11. Most likely to snatch something without asking, say
12. Tinder's flame, e.g.
13. Slimy green
14. Kvass grains
22. "Mmm!"
23. Obscure record producer?
26. Lou of indie rock band Sebadoh (whose name inverted means a minimal standard)
27. China Clipper carrier
28. Spartan square
29. "Rules," in Spanish
31. Made a big-picture assessment (of)
32. Fix up, as a doc
33. "Oleo" composer Rollins
36. They're so crazy they just might work (one hopes)
39. Strand purchase
40. Make like a moonstone
45. Plaque + time
47. "I tell ___ where to put it, never tell ___ where I'm 'bout to be" ("WAP" lyric)
49. Bellini opera parodied by Ibsen
51. Club relatives
52. More than a step
53. Handy command
55. "Nothing is stronger than habit" writer
56. Captain's command
57. Empire State Building bulbs
59. Onsen, e.g.

COPYEDITING THE CLASSICS

by Caitlin Van Dusen

THE GREAT GATSBY (1925)
by F. SCOTT FITZGERALD

Most of the big shore places were closed now and there were hardly any lights except the shadowy, moving glow of a ferry-boat across the Sound. And as the moon rose higher the inessential houses began to melt away until gradually I became aware of the old island here that flowered once for Dutch sailor's eyes—a fresh, green breast of the new world. Its vanished trees, the trees that had made way for Gatsby's house, had once pondered in whispers to the last and greatest of all of human dreams; for a transitory enchanted moment man must have held his breath in the presence of this continent, compelled into an aesthetic contemplation he neither understood or desired, face to face for the last time in history with something commensurate in his capacity for wonder.

And as I sat there brooding on the old, unknown world, I thought of Gatsby's wonder when he first picked out the green light at end of Daisy's dock. He had come along way to this blue lawn, and his dream must have seemed so close that he could hardly fail to grasp it. He did not know that it was already behind him, somewhere back in that vast obscurity beyond the city, where the dark fields of the republic rolled on under the night.

Gatsby believed in the green light, the orgiastic future that year by year recedes before us. It eluded us then, but that's no matter—tomorrow we will run faster, stretch out our arms further… And one fine morning—

So we beat on, boats against the current, born back ceaselessly into the past.   *(answers on page 132)*

JACKET CAPTCHA

CAN YOU IDENTIFY THESE NINE CLASSIC BOOK JACKETS?

COMPLETE ME

HOW WELL DO YOU KNOW GEORGE SAUNDERS? FILL IN THIS PARAGRAPH OF BIOGRAPHICAL TRIVIA, PENNED BY THE AUTHOR HIMSELF.

I was born in A_____, Texas, but I grew up in _____. While in

high school, I worked as a delivery boy for my dad's _____n_, played

_____r, and was prom _____. Seriously. I received a bachelor of science

in geophysical engineering from the Colorado School of Mines, where I was

trained to obtain and analyze se_____ data, in order to prospect for ____.

For two years I worked as a geophysicist in S_____. While there, I became

ill after swimming in a river that had _____ from over one hundred

monkeys in it. On returning home, I worked as a k_____-_____

in a s_____. I published a children's book about the perils of an

economy that relies entirely on the production of _____ _____. The book is

set in the fictional town of _____ and was illustrated by _____ _____,

who also illustrated *The Stinky Cheese Man*.

FOR SALE

HAD TO MOVE OUT OF EX-GF'S APARTMENT—Midcentury modern credenza for sale, teak with cane accents. Good quality. Brooklyn. Too weak to deliver too broke to make rent. Also some wear. Contact *alyseburnside@ gmail.com* if interested.

ALL KINDS OF INTELLECTUAL PROPERTY FOR SALE—Never-before-seen characters (Wiggleman, Dangerio, Noodler, The Force, Emily Oddity, Tom Horrible) PLUS original movie concepts (Big Bad Babies, Big Bad Babies Take Lisbon, Big Bad Babies' Hollywood Easter Musical Mixup) and so many more. *makemeanofferforthisip1922@ gmail.com.*

HELP WANTED

COULD SOMEONE PLEASE—Create an app that allows me to sync a radio broadcast of a basketball game to a television broadcast? I don't have the slightest idea how to go about creating something like that, but maybe someone who reads *The Believer* does. Conservatively, I think an app like this would be worth one billion dollars. Just my opinion.

PRETEND TO BE ME—While feeding a neighborhood crow? I'm looking for someone in the Bay Area to wear a latex mask of my face (I have the mask!) and feed peanuts to a neighborhood crow (who I befriended but now no longer have time in my schedule to feed). They can remember faces and I do not want to let him down! *crowmagnonman@gmail.com.*

SERVICES

BAD BOOK REVIEWS—Can be avoided by good editing. Try us for free! *info@bookhelpline.com.*

GET MEDITATIVE!—Choose bliss! Ride catharsis! Slow that heartbeat! Eschew words! Revel in drone! Google OHYUNG "IMAGINE NAKED!" ♫ ۞•٠•۰◦

CLASSIFIEDS

Believer Classifieds cost $2 per word. They can be placed by emailing classifieds@thebeliever.net. All submissions subject to editorial approval. No results guaranteed.

FREELANCE TRIP SITTER—Seeks drug users to keep track of. Looking to do new drugs in a new situation? I'll make sure no one claws their eyeballs out or freaks and calls the cops. Ask about rates for larger groups (great for weird anniversaries or desert college graduations). **415-DAY-TRIP.**

FELICITATIONS

CHIARAThanksForCallingMeBack

DEAR CHARLOTTE AND MARC. Thank you for subscribing to *The Believer* for me. <3. **BARAK KASSAR**.

CONGRATULATIONS ON THE WEDDING—Nayantara & Paolo! A *Believer* subscription was not on the registry but hope you enjoy it nevertheless :). **TITA.**

HEY S.—Without a grand plan, day after day we traveled yahaan and vahaan found friendships, sublets, and a cat—What's next—who knows—keep walking with me? <3 **SAHAR.**

CARRIE BROWNSTEIN—If you're reading, I loved *Portlandia*. Season 4 was my favorite. **LENA.**

MISSED CONNECTIONS

SEEKING—Man at Paris Baguette in Chinatown, NY on January 6, 2023. You were wearing blue corduroy pants and a varsity jacket with the Mario Kart logo on it, and carrying a copy of *The Believer*. Please don't get the wrong idea: I'm not interested in you, just the jacket you were wearing. Very cool jacket. I need it in my life. Please write back through this Classifieds page. **CHAD.**

SUBMISSIONS

SUBMIT YOUR MANUSCRIPT—To the 2023 Maxy Book Awards (*www.maxyawards.com*) for a chance to win $1,500! The Maxy Awards donates a large part of its proceeds directly to the Home of the Innocents to help those families that need it most.

PINEROW.COM—publish your poetry.

PUBLICATIONS

WRITERS/READERS—Who have had enough of the same-old-same-old and crave interesting short stories: two printings of *Coolest American Stories 2022* sold out completely in less than a year's time, and *Coolest American Stories 2023*, which features an uncollected story by Morgan Talty is already inspiring writers to write fearlessly: *www. amzn.to/3VunhLD.* Order a copy and then maybe submit your own extraordinary story: *www.coolestamericanstories.com.*

COST OF PAPER!—An unprintable publication. *costofpaper.com.*

BEAUTIFUL MACHINE WOMAN LANGUAGE—Poems by Catherine Chen, forthcoming Noemi Press, fall 2023.

A DEMONIC CRYSTAL RADIO—A single mom crushing on a warlock while trying to save the day. A weirded-out fisherman searching for his favorite deckhand—missing under spooky circumstances. *Kill Radio*, a novel by Lauren Bolger. Coming April 2023 from Malarkey Books. *malarkeybooks.com/store/ killradio.*

SLAB IS SEEKING—Your oddest and best fiction, creative nonfiction, poetry, and text-based art for our upcoming issue #18. Algorithm-free reading done by real humans and a pet sloth named Rocky. Submission info/back issues at *slablitmag.org.*

WHAT IS FEELING?—What is melancholy? Can language translate either? 回 / *Return* by Emily Lee Luan, Nightboat Books, April 2023. Preorder at *nightboat.org.*

Illustrations by Tomi Um

INTERNATIONAL BESTSELLER LISTS

See what the rest of the world is reading in this regular feature, which highlights a rotating cast of countries in each issue.

COMPILED BY GINGER GREENE AND ALEXANDER ROTHSTEIN,
ACCORDING TO 2022 ANNUAL LISTS

SPAIN

1. *Todo va a mejorar* (***Everything Is Going to Get Better***) **by Almudena Grandes.** *The last novel written by Grandes before her death depicts a Spain of the near future, governed by technocrats and in the throes of a deadly pandemic.*

2. *Las madres* (***The Mothers***) **by Carmen Mola.** *Inspector Elena Blanco works to solve the case of two murdered men whose bodies were both discovered with an implanted fetus.*

3. *Esclava de la libertad* (***Slave of Freedom***) **by Ildefonso Falcones.** *Set in colonial Cuba and twenty-first century-Spain, this novel tells the story of two Black women fighting the same wealthy family for freedom and racial justice.*

4. *El caso Alaska Sanders* (***The Alaska Sanders Affair***) **by Joël Dicker.** *An anonymous letter causes Sergeant Perry Gahalowood to question the conclusion of a decade-old case he thought he had solved.*

5. *Violeta* (***Violet***) **by Isabel Allende.** *Violeta del Valle imparts sage wisdom as she recounts her hundred-year life in a letter to her grandson.*

6. *La gran serpiente* (***The Great Serpent***) **by Pierre Lemaitre.** *The skilled sixty-three-year-old assassin Mathilde runs into trouble as her memory deteriorates.*

7. *Aniquilación* (***Annihilation***) **by Michel Houllebecq.** *A novel about politics and family life, set in France during the election season of 2027.*

8. *La ladrona de huesos* (***The Bone Thief***) **by Manel Loureiro.** *An amnesiac must steal relics from the Cathedral of Santiago to save the life of the one person who can help her regain her memory.*

9. *La familia* (***The Family***) **by Sara Mesa.** *A complicated portrayal of the strictures and secrecy of a family, following its six members and told over decades.*

10. *Revolución* (***Revolution***) **by Arturo Pérez-Reverte.** *The Spanish mining engineer Martín Garrett Ortiz undergoes a personal journey against the backdrop of the Mexican Revolution.*

NORWAY

1. *Å vanne blomster om kvelden* (***Fresh Water for Flowers***) **by Valérie Perrin.** *A cemetery groundskeeper, whose life is described in flashbacks, has the chance to learn of her vanished husband's whereabouts.*

2. *Blodmåne* (***Blood Moon***) **by Jo Nesbø.** *Weathered detective Harry Hole works with a team of misfits to rescue an aging actress being held hostage by a drug cartel.*

3. *Det ender med oss* (***It Ends with Us***) **by Colleen Hoover.** *Lily enters a relationship with a charming but noncommittal man and is confronted with memories of a past relationship.*

4. *21 års grense* (***21-year limit***) **by Frode Øverli.** *An installment in the comic strip series Pondus, starring the eponymous football enthusiast and pub owner as he and his family find themselves in various predicaments.*

5. *Kongeriket* (***The Kingdom***) **by Jo Nesbø.** *Upon a man's return to the rural village of his childhood, tensions rise between him and his brother when the case of their deceased parents is reopened.*

6. *Den savnede søsteren* (***The Missing Sister***) **by Lucinda Riley.** *Using the only clue they have—the image of an emerald ring—six sisters search for their seventh sister.*

7. *Når hvalene synger* (***Silver Bay***) **by Jojo Moyes.** *A romance blooms with the arrival of a new guest at a seaside hotel.*

8. *Forræderen* (***The Traitor***) **by Jørn Lier Horst.** *While investigating a mysterious death in the wake of a landslide, a detective suspects police corruption.*

9. *Jente, 1983* (***Girl, 1983***) **by Linn Ullmann.** *Forty years later, a woman works through her fragmented memory of an experience she had at the age of sixteen.*

10. *Havets kirkegård* (***The Sea's Cemetery***) **by Aslak Nore.** *The suicide of her grandma prompts a woman to uncover her family history, beginning with the shipwreck that killed her grandfather.*

INDIA

1. ***War of Lanka*** **by Amish Tripathi.** *The three protagonists of the Ram Chandra series prepare for war in India in 3400 BCE.*

2. ***400 Days*** **by Chetan Bhagat.** *In this romantic thriller, two detectives help the beautiful Alia try to find her missing daughter.*

3. ***One Arranged Murder*** **by Chetan Bhagat.** *When a detective's fiancée is murdered on the day of Karva Chauth, he and his colleague try to find the killer.*

4. *Ret Samadhi* (***Tomb of Sand***) **by Geetanjali Shree.** *An eighty-year-old woman emerges from her depression and returns to Pakistan with her daughter.*

5. ***You Only Live Once*** **by Stuti Changle.** *A YouTuber, a comedian, and a beach-shack owner search for a famous singer who has disappeared in Goa.*

6. ***The Girl in Room 105*** **by Chetan Bhagat.** *A man receives a text inviting him to the hostel room of his ex-girlfriend, only to find her dead upon his arrival.*

7. ***The Bird with Golden Wings*** **by Sudha Murty.** *A collection of fantastical short stories by Murty, an award-winning author and educator.*

8. ***That Night*** **by Nidhi Upadhyay.** *Twenty years after the death of a hostel-mate, four friends from college begin to receive anonymous threats.*

9. ***One Day, Life Will Change*** **by Saranya Umakanthan.** *After a difficult marriage, the recently divorced Samaira falls in love with a successful entrepreneur.*

10. ***Something I Never Told You*** **by Shravya Bhinder.** *This love story begins when a shy teenager becomes enamored with the girl who moves into his grandmother's house.*

CANADA

1. ***Five Little Indians*** **by Michelle Good.** *After being separated from their families at a young age, survivors of a Canadian Indian residential school grapple with their trauma.*

2. ***Finding the Mother Tree*** **by Suzanne Simard.** *The author presents a view into the world of trees as live entities capable of complex existences.*

3. ***The Marrow Thieves*** **by Cherie Dimaline.** *An Indigenous teenager navigates a dystopian world where Indigenous people are hunted for their bone marrow.*

4. ***21 Things You May Not Know about the Indian Act: Helping Canadians Make Reconciliation with Indigenous Peoples a Reality*** **by Bob Joseph.** *The author details the effects the 1876 Indian Act has had on the lives of generations of Indigenous people.*

5. ***Scarborough*** **by Catherine Hernandez.** *This novel describes the troubles of members of an economically disadvantaged Toronto community.*

6. ***The Maid*** **by Nita Prose.** *After her grandmother dies, Molly Gray starts work as a maid, and soon finds herself a suspect in the murder of a wealthy man found dead in a hotel suite.*

7. ***The Barren Grounds*** **by David A. Robertson.** *Two Indigenous children discover a portal in the attic of their foster home that transports them to another reality.*

8. ***Sea of Tranquility*** **by Emily St. John Mandel.** *The separate but occasionally interconnected adventures of several people, including an exiled teenager, a famous writer, and a detective.*

9. ***Ducks: Two Years in the Oil Sands*** **by Kate Beaton.** *This autobiographical graphic novel follows the author's life after moving to Alberta to work in the oil sands mining industry.*

10. ***The Sleeping Car Porter*** **by Suzette Mayr.** *In 1929, Baxter, a closeted Black man working as a train car porter, harbors dreams of one day becoming a dentist.*

NOTES ON OUR CONTRIBUTORS

Aria Aber is a writer based in Los Angeles. Her poems have appeared in *The New Yorker*, *The New Republic*, Poem-a-Day, and elsewhere. Her first book of poems, *Hard Damage* (University of Nebraska Press, 2019), won a Whiting Award. She has been granted fellowships from New York University, the Wisconsin Institute of Creative Writing, and Kundiman, as well as the Wallace Stegner Fellowship at Stanford University. She is currently pursuing a PhD at the University of Southern California.

Andrea Bajani is an award-winning Italian novelist and poet. His novel *If You Kept a Record of Sins*, translated by Elizabeth Harris and published in the United States by Archipelago Books, won the Super Mondello Prize, the Brancati Prize, the Recanati Prize, and the Lo Straniero Prize. His latest novel, *Il libro delle case* (The book of homes), was finalist for the Strega Prize and the Campiello Prize, and is being published in more than seventeen countries. It will be published in the United States by Deep Vellum. He is currently the distinguished writer in residence at Rice University in Houston.

Gabrielle Bell has contributed to *The New Yorker*, *The Paris Review*, *McSweeney's Quarterly*, and *VICE*. Her first full-length graphic memoir, *Everything Is Flammable*, was named one of the best graphic novels of 2017 by *Entertainment Weekly*, *Paste*, and *Publisher's Weekly*. Her most recent work, *Career Shoplifter*, is a collection of comics about and drawings of New York City café life. She lives in Brooklyn, New York.

Hayden Bennett is a writer, artist, and musician living in Southern California.

Alexander Chee is most recently the author of *How To Write An Autobiographical Novel* and the editor of *Best American Essays 2022*. He lives in Vermont and teaches creative writing at Dartmouth College.

Yvonne Conza's writing has appeared in *Longreads*, *AGNI*, *BOMB*, *Los Angeles Review of Books*, *Catapult*, *The Rumpus*, *Joyland*, *Blue Mesa Review*, and other publications. She is the coauthor of the user-friendly dog-training guide *Training for Both Ends of the Leash* (Penguin Random House).

Danielle Dutton's most recent books are the novel *Margaret the First* and the illustrated nonfiction chapbook *A Picture Held Us Captive*. Her fiction and criticism have appeared in *The New Yorker*, *The Paris Review*, *Bomb*, *Music & Literature*, *Harper's Magazine*, and elsewhere.

Ricardo Frasso Jaramillo is a poet and writer. His work can be found in *The New York Times*, *McSweeney's Quarterly*, *The Rumpus*, and *The Adroit Journal*, among other venues. He is a 2022–23 National Book Critics Circle Emerging Critic and a case manager at Oakland International High School, which serves recently arrived immigrant youth in the Oakland Unified School District.

Dave Eggers is the author of *The Circle*, *The Every*, and *The Museum of Rain*, among other books.

Ginger Greene is a writer from Toronto.

Elizabeth Harris's recent translations from the Italian include works by Andrea Bajani, Francesco Pacifico, Claudia Durastanti, and Antonio Tabucchi for Archipelago Books, Riverhead Books, Fitzcarraldo Editions, Text Publishing, and Farrar, Straus and Giroux. Her grants and prizes include a National Endowment for the Arts translation fellowship, a PEN America translation grant, the Italian Prose in Translation Award, and the National Translation Award.

Brandon Hobson is the author of four novels, most recently *The Removed*. His novel *Where the Dead Sit Talking* was a finalist for the National Book Award and won the Reading the West Book Award, among other distinctions. His middle-grade book, *The Storyteller*, will be out from Scholastic in May 2023. His short stories have won a Pushcart Prize and have appeared in *The Best American Short Stories*, *McSweeney's Quarterly*, *Conjunctions*, *NOON*, and elsewhere. He teaches creative writing at New Mexico State University and in the low-residency MFA program at the Institute of American Indian Arts. Hobson is an enrolled citizen of the Cherokee Nation of Oklahoma.

Zoë Hu has written for *The New Republic*, *The Baffler*, and *The Nation*.

Melissa Locker is a writer and music podcast impresario in the making. She lives on the internet and runs on coffee. You can follow her at @woolyknickers but not in real life.

Mara Naselli is a writer, editor, and recipient of the 2014 Rona Jaffe Writers' Foundation Award. Her work has appeared in *AGNI*, *The Kenyon Review*, *The Hudson Review*, and elsewhere. She lives in Michigan.

Leslie Carol Roberts is the author of two books about travel, culture, and ecological thought: *The*

Entire Earth and Sky: Views on Antarctica (2012) and *Here Is Where I Walk: Episodes from a Life in the Forest* (2019). Her work has appeared in *Fast Company* and *The Nation*, among other places. In 2018 she founded the Ecopoesis Project with two architects; they host gatherings of shared ecological thought and art-making focused on increased solidarity, as humans and more-than-humans face climate change together.

Rebecca Rukeyser is the author of *The Seaplane on Final Approach*. She teaches creative writing at Bard College Berlin.

Ross Scarano is a writer and editor from Pittsburgh, and his work has appeared in *Complex*, *Billboard*, *The Wall Street Journal*, *The Ringer*, *SSENSE*, *GQ*, and other publications. He lives in Brooklyn, New York.

Meara Sharma is a writer, artist, and producer whose work has appeared in *Frieze*, *Guernica*, *Ambit*, *VICE*, *The New York Times*, *The Washington Post*, and elsewhere. With roots in Massachusetts and India, she currently lives in London.

Azareen Van der Vliet Oloomi is a novelist and essayist. Her novel *Call Me Zebra* won the 2019 PEN/Faulkner Award and was longlisted for the PEN Open Book Award. She is the recipient of a Whiting Award and a National Book Foundation 5 Under 35 Award. She lives in New York City and in South Bend, Indiana.

Noah Van Sciver is a multiple-award-winning cartoonist who first came to comics readers' attention with his Eisner Award–nominated comic book series *Blammo*. His work has appeared in *The New Yorker*, *Wired*, and *Mad* magazine, as well as in many graphic anthologies. Van Sciver has written and drawn numerous graphic novels, including the Fante Bukowski series for Fantagraphics and *Joseph Smith and the Mormons* (Abrams Books, 2022).

Jenny Xie is the author of the poetry collections *Eye Level* and *The Rupture Tense* and the chapbook *Nowhere to Arrive*. She lives in New York City and teaches at Bard College.

Emily Jungmin Yoon is the author of *A Cruelty Special to Our Species* and *Ordinary Misfortunes*, the 2017 winner of the Sunken Garden Chapbook Prize by Tupelo Press (selected by Maggie Smith). Also a translator, she has published *Against Healing: Nine Korean Poets*, a chapbook of poems by Korean women writers.

Molly Young is a book critic at *The New York Times*.

IN THE NEXT ISSUE

Not all contents are guaranteed; replacements will be satisfying

Adaptive Fiction . . . . TED MCDERMOTT
A profile of Donald D. Hoffman, the cognitive scientist who doesn't believe he has a brain.

Mount Fear Diary . . . . JOSHUA HUNT
On a work trip in Japan, and unable to return to his ancestral village in Alaska to mourn the loss of his favorite uncle, the author travels to Osore-zan—or "Mount Fear"—an active volcano that is believed to be a portal to the underworld.

Even Their Memory . . . . SAHAR DELIJANI
How the Iranian massacre of 1988, in which thousands of political prisoners were killed, shapes the anti-government protests of today.

SOLUTIONS TO THIS ISSUE'S GAMES AND PUZZLES

CROSSWORD
(Page 124)

COPYEDITING THE CLASSICS
(Page 125)

Most of the big shore places were closed now and there were hardly any lights except the shadowy, moving glow of a ferryboat across the Sound. And as the moon rose higher the inessential houses began to melt away until gradually I became aware of the old island here that flowered once for Dutch sailor's (1) eyes—a fresh, green breast of the new world. Its vanished trees, the trees that had made way for Gatsby's house, had once pondered (2) in whispers to the last and greatest of all of (3) human dreams; for a transitory enchanted moment man must have held his breath in the presence of this continent, compelled into an aesthetic contemplation he neither understood or (4) desired, face to face for the last time in history with something commensurate in (5) his capacity for wonder.

And as I sat there brooding on the old, unknown world, I thought of Gatsby's wonder when he first picked out the green light at (6) end of Daisy's dock. He had come along (7) way to this blue lawn, and his dream must have seemed so close that he could hardly fail to grasp it. He did not know that it was already behind him, somewhere back in that vast obscurity beyond the city, where the dark fields of the republic rolled on under the night.

Gatsby believed in the green light, the orgiastic (8) future that year by year recedes before us. It eluded us then, but that's no matter—tomorrow we will run faster, stretch out our arms further... (9) And one fine morning—

So we beat on, boats against the current, born (10) back ceaselessly into the past.

(1) sailors': The possessive apostrophe follows the *s* that pluralizes *sailors*. (2) pandered: The verb *pander* means "to cater to and often exploit the weaknesses of others"; the verb *ponder* means "to deliberate over." The first is meant here. (3) all: Delete *of*. *Of* should be deleted except when it precedes a non-possessive pronoun (all of us). (4) nor: *neither* and *nor* work as a pair; when *neither* is used, *nor* must follow. (5) commensurate to: The adjective *commensurate*, which means "proportionate," is used with *to* or *with*. (6) the: Missing short words such as *the* are often overlooked. (7) a long: Mistaking *along* for a *long* is a commonly overlooked typo. (8) orgastic: *Orgiastic* means "tending to produce wild emotion, or having the qualities of an orgy"; *orgastic* means "of, relating to, or being an orgasm or orgy." Fitzgerald intended the latter here. (9) farther: *Farther* is used for physical, measurable distance; *further* is used for metaphorical distance. (10) borne: *Born* is used only as an adjective or in the passive-voice verb *to be born*. *Borne* is the past participle of the verb *bear*, which means "to transport," used in the passive voice here.

JACKET CAPTCHA
(Page 126)

1. *The Great Gatsby* by F. Scott Fitzgerald
2. *Portnoy's Complaint* by Philip Roth
3. *Slaughterhouse-Five* by Kurt Vonnegut
4. *Herzog* by Saul Bellow
5. *The Catcher in the Rye* by J. D. Salinger
6. *Millions of Cats* by Wanda Gág
7. *My Year of Rest and Relaxation* by Ottessa Moshfegh
8. *Of Mice and Men* by John Steinbeck
9. *White Teeth* by Zadie Smith

COMPLETE ME
(Page 127)

I was born in **Amarillo**, Texas, but I grew up in **Chicago**. While in high school, I worked as a delivery boy for my dad's **restaurant**, played **guitar**, and was prom **king**. Seriously. I received a bachelor of science in geophysical engineering from the Colorado School of Mines, where I was trained to obtain and analyze **seismic** data, in order to prospect for **oil**. For two years I worked as a geophysicist in **Sumatra**. While there, I became ill after swimming in a river that had **poop** from over one hundred monkeys in it. On returning home, I worked as a **knuckle-puller** in a **slaughterhouse**. I published a children's book about the perils of an economy that relies entirely on the production of **goats' milk**. The book is set in the fictional town of **Frip** and was illustrated by **Lane Smith**, who also illustrated *The Stinky Cheese Man*.